D1617396

ALFRED ADLER, THE FORGOTTEN PROPHET

A Vision for the 21st Century

Loren Grey

 PRAEGER

Westport, Connecticut
London

Library of Congress Cataloging-in-Publication Data

Grey, Loren.
    Alfred Adler, the forgotten prophet : a vision for the 21st
century / Loren Grey.
        p.   cm.
    Includes bibliographical references and index.
    ISBN 0–275–96072–2 (alk. paper)
    1. Adlerian psychology.   2. Psychoanalysis—History.   3. Adler,
Alfred, 1870–1937.   I. Title.
    BF175.G734   1998
    150.19'53—dc21   97–40885

British Library Cataloguing in Publication Data is available.

Library of Congress Catalog Card Number: 97–40885
ISBN: 0–275–96072–2

First published in 1998

Praeger Publishers, 88 Post Road West, Westport, CT 06881
An imprint of Greenwood Publishing Group, Inc.

Printed in the United States of America

The paper used in this book complies with the
Permanent Paper Standard issued by the National
Information Standards Organization (Z39.48–1984).

10 9 8 7 6 5 4 3 2 1

Copyright Acknowledgments

The author and publisher gratefully acknowledge permission for use of the following
material:

Selected excerpts from *The Individual Psychology of Alfred Adler* by Heinz L. Ansbacher
and Rowena R. Ansbacher. Copyright © 1956 by Basic Books, Inc. Copyright renewed 1984
by Heinz L. and Rowena R. Ansbacher. Reprinted by permission of Basic Books, a division
of HarperCollins Publishers, Inc.

Selected excerpts from *The New Psychology of Dreaming* by Richard M. Jones (New York:
Grune & Stratten, 1970). Reprinted by permission of W. B. Saunders Co., a Division of
Harcourt Brace and Co.

Contents

Preface

The why of things has always fascinated me. When I was first exposed to Adlerian psychology more than fifty years ago, I was intrigued by its premises, though as a therapy client in the earliest years I was more concerned with solving my own problems than delving into the mysteries of Adler's ideas, particularly about social interest. It was many years before I began to explore Adlerian theory with the idea of using it professionally. Yet, I always felt that the social implications of his theories were literally earth shattering. Here, to me, was an answer for many of the world's problems.

During those years I learned that many of Adler's concepts seem superficially simple, but most are far more complex than has really been known.

As we continue to probe into the mysteries of the human mind, it seems appropriate to recall that many of Alfred Adler's early supporters felt that he was one hundred years ahead of his time. Now at the brink of the new millennium, this book is an attempt to assess the nature of his thinking and how it squares with what his followers said.

Though many of his supplemental concepts are in wide use today as part of other psychological disciplines (i.e., transactional analysis and reality therapy, as well as the earlier theories of Karen Horney and Harry Stack Sullivan, to mention a few) there are still others that have not yet been fully clarified or comprehended today.

Perhaps one of the most important of these ideas occurred in 1911, shortly after Adler's break with Freud. He started a new movement which he called "the psychology of the undivided whole." Of course holism, as such, is not a new concept, nor was it then. It means that the whole is greater than the sum of its parts and therefore the whole cannot be deduced by adding up the parts; also, a portion of the whole can be found in each part. However, in this case it was the first time that an attempt was made to apply this concept to human psychological behavior. In Adler's view, all the components of our mind and body cooperate, impelling us to move toward a mythical and at the same time unattainable "goal of perfection." The meaning of this goal is unique to the individual, but has been expressed in superlatives such as being the best, the worst, the tallest, the brightest, and so forth.

Some ten years later, another thinker—this time in a different realm—named J. C. Smuts, former Premier of South Africa, wrote a book entitled *Holism and Evolution* [66].* In this bold new volume, he suggested that the entire cosmos was in a state of holistic evolutionary development, the principle of which was to move toward a greater holism and greater diversity. In his view we have progressed from the gases of interstellar space to the rocks and rivers of Earth and perhaps other planets, toward organic development (which to him was a direct outgrowth of inorganic material), to the highest form, which is human consciousness. For him, all of this was, in a sense, preordained by the holistic principle.

Except for Adler's mention of Smuts and the support of his ideas a few years later, like so many great misunderstood concepts throughout the years, this one nearly vanished without a trace. However, some years later a thinker in a totally disparate field, the brilliant physicist David Bohm, again cited Smuts as having ideas analogous to his own. In this case, however, Bohm, who was a friend of and collaborator with Albert Einstein, had proposed a dramatic new concept in the field of quantum physics. In it he felt there was a holistic principle underlying what he called the "explicate order," which governed the movement of electrons and molecules. This he called the "implicate order," which somehow involved all of the particles and objects which, in a holistic fashion, moved in their mysterious ways through space.

Later he began to apply some of these ideas to a new area: human consciousness. This led him far away from many of his colleagues and toward new groups, among them being the Indian seer, J. Krishnamurti. His association with Krishnamurti was stimulating at first, but apparently did not produce what he was looking for, and eventually their relationship ended.

In my view, during his later years Bohm was not able to fully apply what he had formulated to this new field—he died in 1992. He had reached a point where he considered objective reality—which is what to him all senses make of the universe around us—to exist as separately from human perception. He called this his "explicate order." There was, however, another aspect of the cosmos which he called the "implicate order," what one might call the infinite. To him, this was an intangible, but still all-powerful pervasive energy or spirit that infuses all living creatures and never dies.

Yet, at the same time, Bohm was deeply puzzled at what he perceived as a "systemic fault" existing in human thought that led to incoherence in the functioning of the ego and did not appear to conform to his implicate order. Had Bohm known more of Adler's view on the thinking process he might have arrived at some very different views than those with which he struggled during the last years of his life. Adler saw our thinking process as completely logical, purposive, coherent, and con-

---

* Throughout the book, bracketed numbers refer to the Bibliography.

forming entirely to the principles of holism in a mind not incapacitated by disability or disease. No matter how mistaken, bizarre, or even psychotic a person's goal and his subsequent behavior, to Adler his attempts to reach that goal were essentially inherent and logical. He called this process "private logic."

In his later years Bohm formed and conducted so-called dialogue groups, which were not like encounter groups but rather largely exchanges of ideas. From them he did come to the belief that there might be such a thing as "collective intelligence" in these groups that could not be attributed to the behavior of a single individual in the group. This "group sense" I have often noted as being present in my practicum group classes at California State University, Northridge (CSUN), and in my view is a function of the holistic process.

Though neither Adler or Bohm have given us a truly definitive answer as to what "thought" or even "holism" really are, this book does, I believe, move us closer to a comprehension of how human thought works. It should also help us to understand more clearly the relationship between the so-called unconscious and conscious minds, which Adler saw as levels of awareness rather than disparate entities as proposed by Freud. Perhaps reading this book may also help those entering the new millennium to have a greater understanding of the nature of personality.

There are of course many among us who assert with cosmic finality that all of this was created by God and there is no need to go further in trying to ascertain why any of this phenomena exists. If we all believed this implicitly it would certainly be comforting, but we would probably know a great deal less about the universe than we do now. Is it possible to believe in such a God and ask these questions? I cannot truthfully answer this because I have always wanted to know why anything and everything exists or happens. If such a God is all-powerful, why does He allow the human race to abuse one another to the extent that we do? On the other hand, if God is a principle rather than an entity, as Smuts appears to suggest, both Adler's as well as some of Bohm's ideas can make a great deal of sense.

However, mastering the intricacies of such ideas was another matter. My first teacher was Lydia Sicher, who received her medical degree from the University of Vienna in 1916, being one of the first women to achieve this honor. Sicher was a brilliant lecturer and writer, but not always easy to understand. However, I did learn most of the clinical aspects of Adler's system—which is far more complex than it seems on the surface—from her, as well as from my reading of Adler's books.

However, the person to whom I am the most indebted for insight into the real dynamics behind Adler's thinking is Rudolf Dreikurs. My initial exposure to his ideas was at a summer series of classes held at the University of Oregon in Eugene in 1959. I was literally electrified by what I learned that summer. Not only this book, but four other books came out of that experience—two in collaboration with Dreikurs titled *Logical Consequences: A New Approach to Discipline* [33], and *A Parents' Guide to Child Discipline* [35], along with two later ones, *Discipline Without Tyranny: Child Training During the First Five Years* [78], and *Discipline Without Fear: Child Training During the Early School Years* [79].

However, what I saw as a structure that helps a person understand Adler and gives him the tools to better use his ideas, I now see as a reinterpretation of some of Adler's original thinking. When Dreikurs first started his Chicago Child Guidance Centers and his Chicago-based training institute, there were considerable controversies about his ideas, some quite heated between him and those of the classical Adlerian school, of which Sicher, Alexandra and Kurt Adler, and Heinz and Rowena Ansbacher were the leaders. To them, Dreikurs's simplification and reinterpretation of Adler's concepts was nearly heretical. The controversy has long since died down as Dreikurs has become more accepted, and this book is an attempt to reconcile what to me are complimentary rather than antagonistic concepts.

Along with this, I have added some of my own ideas from my years of experience in working with adults and children. A complicating factor in all this has been the emergence of a new biography of Adler entitled *The Drive for Self: Alfred Adler and the Fundamentals of Individual Psychology* by Edward Hoffman [46], which has resulted in my correcting a few errors I had put forth earlier about Adler, based on what I had read in earlier biographies by Phyllis Bottome and Hertha Orgler.

Perhaps what I learned the most from Hoffman's book was that most of Adler's theoretical ideas emerged through his association with Freud. Freud's concept that ideas out of consciousness influence behavior opened a new door in our understanding of the human psyche. I have always felt that, unfortunately for him, what Freud saw beyond that door, he did not really understand—but Adler did. My guess as to why this happened is that Freud was essentially autocratic in nature and Adler was democratic. When Adler convinced himself that neurosis was the result of mistaken perceptions of social relationships with others (which was a *learned* behavior, mostly from environmental influences, and could be unlearned, rather than the result of instinctual sexual drives as Freud had proposed), in my view a major new direction began in our understanding of human nature.

This book is an attempt to acquaint those who are unfamiliar with Adler's ideas with how these concepts came about and what they essentially mean. I see it as "Adler + Sicher + Dreikurs + Grey," with some help in the child's developmental process from the French psychologist, Jean Piaget. As always, when one attempts to describe another's theories, one's own ideas usually end up being embedded in the results.

I am indebted to many other people who have helped me, either knowingly or unknowingly in the preparation of this book. I am indebted to Jon Tuska, who has pushed me into rewriting portions of the text which he said were needed. If this book is finally published, he was right. I am most grateful for the tremendous efforts and helpful suggestions of my wife, Bonnie. But my greatest appreciation is to my loyal secretary and dear friend, Katharine Haggerty, who, in addition to help with content, has gone through the endless hours and hours of typing the revisions—easier now because of the computer, but still time consuming. To Bonnie and Kathy I dedicate this book.

Chapter One

Who Was Alfred Adler?

He was born in Rudolfsheim, Austria, a small village near Vienna on February 7, 1870, the second of six children. His father was a grain merchant of modest means who had originally come from Burgenland. As a small child he was not robust. He had rickets and a spasm of the epiglottis when he became angry, which often created severe shortness of breath. When he was four years old, one of his brothers died in the bed next to him. At the age of five he nearly died himself from an attack of pneumonia. Apparently from this illness may have come an early decision to become a doctor—an ambition that was eagerly supported, even pushed, by his parents. In a sense, his own life was a vindication of one of his earliest concepts—intellectual compensation over physical inferiorities. As an adult he was a rotund little man with a small mustache and large, beautiful expressive eyes peering out from behind wire-rimmed glasses. Even today, this astonishing little man's theories are not really very well known by most students of psychology. Yet directly or indirectly, he may have influenced our understanding of human nature as much as or more than any one individual in this century. His name was Alfred Adler.

EARLY SOCIAL INFLUENCES

In his early years there was little in his career that would portend the astounding development of his masterly system. Though Adler was a gregarious boy and had many friends, his enrollment at the age of ten into the *Gymnasium*, the preparatory school for entrance to the Medical School at the University of Vienna, was not auspicious. He found the academic competition very difficult, particularly in mathematics, and actually failed and was required to repeat his first year. His father threatened to remove him from the *Gymnasium* and make him a shoemaker's apprentice. This threat, though probably far-fetched, apparently frightened him enough so that his grades improved markedly. Though he admitted later that he had never liked the *Gymnasium*, he worked hard enough to obtain his certificate and was accepted to the Medical School at the University of Vienna in 1888.

His entrance into medical school was a great turning point in his life. The curriculum—which emphasized experimentation and diagnostic exactitude rather than interest in patients—bored him for the most part. He was particularly frustrated by the long hours of study and was much happier socializing with his friends at the nearby cafes in Vienna; and over the years, only barely managed to obtain the grades necessary to graduate on 22 November 1895.

There in the cafes was where he began to formulate his ideas about equality and social relationships; not in the formal dreary walls of college, but in endless evenings of lively discussions with his friends and colleagues about problems of the day. In medical school he received no formal training in psychiatry; his only exposure to anything related to the field was his taking of a course called "The Diseases of the Nervous System" by Richard von Kraft Ebbing. Just before he obtained his medical degree, he became a volunteer in ophthalmology, at a clinic run for poor parents named the Poliknilik. It was here, with impoverished patients, that he began to develop his strong commitments to the concept of socialism in regard to social issues. Though he counted the young Leon Trotsky among his friends, and married a Russian girl, Raissa Epstein, who became an avid follower of Trotsky for many years, Adler himself never endorsed Communism and even went so far as to blast the repressive tactics of imposing socialism by force by Lenin, Trotsky, and his followers during and after the Russian Revolution of 1917. Still, his strong commitment to the social well-being of others may have been the most important part of his thinking that led to the break between him and Sigmund Freud in 1911.

It is well known that the psychological system of Sigmund Freud, which had only been formalized some years before Adler became associated with Freud, swept the medical, and then most of the psychological, world between 1920 and 1950. Up until his first visit to the United States in 1925, Adler's theories were little known—at least in the United States.

However, when he first came to America, a number of his theories—particularly those revolving around the compensation and overcompensation for inferiority feelings—became widely accepted, except of course for the medical establishment, which was completely dominated by the followers of Freud. The term "inferiority complex" became for a time a household word.

WHY ARE THERE SO FEW BOOKS ON ADLER IN PRINT TODAY?

Why is it then that today there are virtually no new books about Adler's ideas in general circulation, though one can find dozens describing in great detail the theories of Freud and Jung?

What may also be puzzling to those who may only have begun to investigate the scope of Adler's thinking, is why he is still so little known to most students of psychology today. Such terms as *unity of the personality*, *teleology*, *organ inferiority*, *masculine protest*, and *social interest* are still not now much better understood, except by Adlerians, than when they were first described by Adler more than sixty years ago. Yet as these subsequent chapters will describe, their relevancy is as immediate as the concept of any modern theorist today. Perhaps one explanation for this phenomenon may be found in what William James once described as the classic stages in the career of a new theory. "Any new theory," said James, "is first attacked as absurd. Then it is admitted to be true but obviously insignificant. Finally, it is seen to be so important that its adversaries claim that they, themselves, have discovered it" [49]. There seems to be little doubt that Adler's theory has passed through the first stage. There are few psychologists with any degree of objectivity today who would consider his concepts absurd, as did Adler's early detractors who were mostly Freudians and, to a somewhat lesser extent behaviorists. Indeed, up until the late 1930s and 1940s, at least some of the new generation of psychologists who were not Freudian or behaviorists somewhat grudgingly admitted that what they knew of it might be true but that it was still considered "superficial" and that his theories dealt only with the present. Other writers claimed he only "dimly" perceived the fundamental aspects of human personality that they now had themselves discovered. Ironically, today, often his theories are underrated because some of his critics say he dealt only with the past.

Indeed, if it had not been for the scholarly reinterpretation and retranslation of much of Adler's writings by Heinz and R. Rowena Ansbacher in their monumental trilogy, *The Individual Psychology of Alfred Adler*, first published in 1956 [18], *Superiority and Social Interest* in 1964 [19], and *Cooperation between the Sexes* in 1978 [20], and the influence of Rudolf Dreikurs and many of his followers, possibly the third state of Adler's theory might never have arrived, at least not in this century. As early as the 1920s and 1930s, there were prominent psychologists and psychiatrists such as Karen Horney, Harry Stack Sullivan, and Erich Fromm, who borrowed heavily from Adler's theories but at the same time calling them their own or labeling themselves "neo-Freudians" rather than "neo-Adlerians," as the Ansbachers themselves suggested they should be called. When Eric Berne wrote *Games People Play,* in which he laid the foundations for transactional analysis, he made little, if any, reference to Adler's thinking. However, few practitioners of transactional analysis today, if pressed, will deny that Adler's system is very much like their own, although the terms are different, and of course they state that they have been "modernized" considerably.

"MORAL" IMPLICATIONS

There are other reasons for the lack of full recognition of the scope of Adler's thinking today. Perhaps one of the most pervasive is that when his system had finally matured, he believed that man, being biologically essentially a social being, was not fully mature psychologically unless he possessed what he called *Gemeinschaftsgefühl*, which has been loosely but perhaps not entirely correctly translated as "social interest," also sometimes called "social feeling," "co-feeling," or "community feeling." Essentially its meaning is that the individual only lives successfully by willing cooperation with others and being deeply concerned with the welfare of others. To Adler, the degree of an individual's psychological maturity depended on how much a person is socially "useful" compared to those considered to be on the socially "useless" side, concerned with their own private purposes. At the same time he asserted that every person is creative but that creativity must be in the useful or cooperative side for the individual to be considered successful in the three basic tasks of life: love, friendship, and work. This of course implies that whatever our personal attempts to evade this or rationalize it, we are essentially fully responsible for our own behavior.

Even if these actions are based on mistaken perceptions which are learned (and can be unlearned), if they are on the uncooperative side, they are considered useless behavior.

Utilization of terms such as these unfortunately imply a moral stance, which suggests that a useful person is considered to be more valuable than a useless one. Of course, Adler, believing as he did in equality of individuals, did not believe anything of the kind, but strongly adhered to what he called the "iron law of coliving" as being a biological and not just social necessity. Those who did not obey this law inevitably suffered some degree of rejection by others but often were able to avoid a full recognition of this consequence by rationalizing its effects through use of defense mechanism.

Most modern psychological systems tend to avoid such terms because they are considered moralistic or perhaps implying religious dogma in describing behavior. Dreikurs has essentially substituted Adler's term "private logic" to "communal logic" to describe these opposites. He also pointed out that though the person's premise might be wrong, the creative behavior of any individual is purposive, organized, and inherently logical, however cooperative or uncooperative it might be.

The changing usage of terms in the mental health field to avoid such "moral" judgments also illustrates this tendency. A *psychopath* now has an *antisocial personality disorder*, *hyperkinesis* in children has been replaced with *attention deficit disorder*. Much of this change in emphasis in terminology has come about because practitioners soon found out that use of words such as "useful" and "useless" or excessive use of psychopathological terms scared away too many of their patients, and so less offensive labels were needed. Even modern Adlerians today operate in terms of "moving away" as against "moving toward" others to define such type of behavior. However, Adlerians still interpret behavior in terms of what the person *wants* rather than what he *is*.

ADLER'S RELATIONSHIP WITH FREUD

But whatever terms are used and/or are acceptable in private practice, Adlerians believe that we *still are fully responsible for our actions*, a fact which has never been popular during any day.

Perhaps another major cause for Adlerians being so unknown today was the relationship between Adler and Freud. Adler was invited to join the Freudian circle, allegedly because he wrote a defense of Freud in a local publication. According to Hoffman, his latest biographer, this written article was never found, but Adler carried the post card he received from Freud around with him for a long time, inviting him to join the group as an equal, and not as a student. Lydia Sicher also told me and others in the Adlerian group in Los Angeles that for a time Adler served as Freud's personal physician, although there is no mention of this in Hoffman's biography. Though Hoffman does not entirely state how joining Freud's circle began the maturing of his own psychological system, it appears that many of his early important concepts evolved from the discussions in this group.

In 1907 Adler published his *Study of Organ Inferiority and Its Psychological Compensation* [1], his first major step in the formulation of his system. The evolution in his thinking from this concept, which started several years before the monograph was published, could be considered a major discovery, but was only more specifically outlined in his later writings. The concept was that we tend to overcompensate not only for real and "alleged" inferiorities, but also for what he called "normal" feelings of inferiority, as well. Such self-regarded deficiencies as too short, too tall, too fat, too thin, or any other aspect of physical or mental development, which are considered by the person to be different therefore inferior but do not interfere with normal physical capacity, may initiate the drive to compensate or overcompensate. However, how we *perceive* this attribute to be different from how we feel others think about it is the essential premise that underlies all of Adlerian theory. These perceptions lead the individual to strive to overcome them, to go from what Adler called a "minus" to a "plus" situation. From this came his original idea which he called "masculine protest," which in turn resulted in what he called a "striving for power," or success, which, due to the prevailing culture, was defined largely in masculine terms.

Though Freud accepted Adler's original idea regarding compensation for organ inferiority, he soon began to see Adler's views about the "sense" or feeling of inferiority as being the basis of psychic development, as a threat to his own long-revered concept that the libido, or infantile sexuality, was the basis of human personality. Adler's further emphasis on birth order and other social influences as a clue to the child's goals, with sex as only a part of that development, became another of the major differences that began to separate the two men. Adler also rejected Freud's notion that the second law of thermodynamics—that of entropy, which states that the degradation of energy occurs according to which a quantity of energy while remaining constant leads to decrease in quality, eventually reaching equilibrium—was applicable to human striving in the form of what Freud termed as the "death wish"—the urge of animate matter to return to the inanimate state. To Adler, at this time the striving was always upward toward life and power, and toward what he called a "future goal of perfection."

In addition, he disputed Freud's theory of the unconscious as being a separate, more or less independent function of the mind apart from consciousness. Adler believed that the so-called unconscious mind was only that part of consciousness of which we are not aware. In his later years he concluded the unconscious was really only the working hypothesis of the psychologist. However, this writer tends to support the views of Dreikurs in denoting the scheme of unconscious versus consciousness as one of "levels of awareness," the nature of which is explained more fully later on.

These and other fundamental differences, many of which may have arisen as the result of temperamental and political clashes between the two men, with Freud behaving as the dominating oldest (although he was really an only child with a brother twenty years his junior), and Adler the rebellious second child. This eventually led to Adler departing from the Freudian circle in 1910 after an eleven to five vote by the Vienna Psychological Society which stated that his views were antithetical to those of the Society. With three followers who left with him, Adler formed his own group which he first called The Independent Society for Psychoanalytical Study. In his final break with Freud in 1913, he changed the name of his enlarged group to The Society for Individual Psychology.

Even this name aroused misconceptions which have endured until this day. The Latin word, *individuum*, which means "undivided," often became mistakenly interpreted as "individual," with the assumption that the basic premise was comparing one's individual differences with those of another. However, Adler named his movement "the psychology of the undivided whole." Also, by the time Adler left Freud and his movement, Freud had become the center of the burgeoning psychiatric discipline. Early in this century, there were only two types of practitioners in the field—doctors and teachers. The few psychologists who did exist were concerned mostly with behavioristic research on animals, and no one else was permitted to practice what was called psychotherapy except physicians at that time. So Adler had almost no early adherents in the medical field.

FREUD AND ADLER AS WRITERS

In addition, Freud was a brilliant writer and managed to capture every nuance and complexity of his system in his wide array of writings. His theories were admirably suited to the medical mystique, as they still are to a considerable extent, even today. It was authoritarian, heavy in emphasis on the benign father figure who took care of all his little children, extremely complex, and difficult to understand. Also, at least in its early stages, the theory of psychoanalysis was based primarily on sex—an idea which was both exciting and at the same time frightening to most of the lay public. Requirements for membership into the Society were severe and demanded a thorough study analysis, which in effect meant that any student who deviated even slightly from a total acceptance of psychoanalysis in his analysis was denied admission to the Society. Adler's system, on the other hand, was less complicated and more egalitarian and at least in its initial phases, not nearly as demanding on students. In the beginning, Adler welcomed almost anyone who wished to join his group.

According to Lydia Sicher, Adler disliked writing intensely. Except for his monumental *The Neurotic Constitution* [2], first published in 1912, but which unfortunately contained his belief in the "will to power" as being the basic motivation in human development, most of his later books were aimed toward the lay public, probably because he realized he could make no real dent in the psychoanalytical movement which dominated the mental health profession during most of the later years of his life. Such books translated into English as *What Life Should Mean to You* [14], and *Social Interest: A Challenge to Mankind* [16], are examples of this.

Adler's books also suffered from severe handicaps, particularly in the English translations which were often made by writers who did not understand psychology thoroughly themselves. They were full of sweeping generalizations, many of which have stood up remarkably well, even to this day, but which offered no explanation or research data to support the dynamics behind them. The tone of Adler's writings in those books, at least in the early translations, appeared to be excessively moralistic, and many of those who read the books felt that the list of "shoulds and oughts" were simply too gargantuan to follow. In addition, Adler offered few specific practical methods for the therapist as to how to deal with his patients. There was much emphasis on what should take place in therapy in general, but little on how it should be done or in suggesting techniques the therapist might use, except in encouraging the patient to help himself in order to help the individual gain insight into his behavior. Ironically, the Ansbachers, in their first definitive clinical text of Adlerian theory, had to rely heavily on these books for insights into Adler's later theories. Nearly all the statements that came from those books they retranslated from the original German and therefore overcame a great many handicaps that were present in the earlier translations. But as we were not at all prepared for social equality even in the 1930s, neither were we prepared for Alfred Adler.

OPPOSITION BY PSYCHOANALYSTS

Psychoanalysis eventually captured the medical profession by storm, except for those few isolated individuals who suggested other disciplines and who struggled through medical school and set up their independent practices. Also, at every opportunity, both Freud and his colleagues set out to deliberately downplay and belittle Adler's ideas as being superficial and not medically sound. There really was no place for Adler or other dissenters to go but to the teachers, whose professional status then was little better than it is today. It is no surprise that the Adlerian movement, mostly under the leadership of Dreikurs, has had its most profound influence on education than on any other field.

Also, though the Adlerian movement did gain adherents after World War II, it was a slow and painful process. Groups were small and almost totally excluded from having any influence on the medical profession, which controlled the mental health movement with an iron hand until many years after the war. Even today, though there are therapists, psychologists, social workers, marriage and family counselors, psychiatry still has enormous control over the mental health movement.

To give one example, usually only psychiatric opinion is accepted as evidence in criminal trials, although this trend is finally beginning to change. In many communities there may be psychologists who are as well or better equipped to render such judgments than psychiatrists, but their opinion is still not commonly accepted in court, except in the interpretation of certain types of tests.

ADLER'S FINAL CONCEPTS

The last major change in Adler's theory occurred after his service as a psychiatrist in the Austrian Army during World War I. He had observed that, frequently, men suffering from severe emotional disturbances as a result of the trauma they suffered in battle still displayed tendencies to bond and strong social feeling that did not appear to come from what he had seen as a striving for power. When he returned to the coffee houses of his beloved Vienna in 1918, he astounded his followers by proposing that the basic human motivation was an "innate predisposition for social interest," one which had to be developed, but which was positive and not negative in nature. Some of his followers could not believe at first what they saw as "love" being proposed as the motive for behavior, rather than power. The basic need of the infant for affection, which Adler had suggested as early as 1908, was later formulated by Dreikurs as evolving into the "need to belong" to others when the child became old enough to perceive that he was a member of a group.

In 1926, Adler coined the final term in his system which he called "styles of life," to describe what he said is "the meaning which individuals give to the world and to themselves," thus, goal, the direction of their striving, and the approaches they make to the problems of life [14]. To Adler, those were all the striving and attitudes the person creatively invents in order to reach his goal.

In the last eleven years of his life, Adler devoted most of his time to teaching, lecturing, and traveling in the United States and England in an almost desperate race to acquaint the world with his teachings in the face of the Holocaust, which he clearly saw emerging. Though his ideas did gain a measure of acceptance outside of the medical and psychiatric profession, his system in its entirety is still not well known, even though many of his concepts are an integral part of most legitimate mental health disciplines today.

SUMMARY OF BASIC ADLERIAN CONCEPTS

Following, in brief terms, are the basic tenets of this system as this writer sees it, with the addition of the interpretations made by other later Adlerians such as Rudolf Dreikurs and Lydia Sicher. To a considerable extent, where research exists concerning these concepts or those related, the weight of evidence has tended to confirm most of the basic theories mentioned previously or in later chapters.

As may be seen, many of these ideas may be familiar to others in the field, but when viewed as part of an holistic system, many of them may seem quite new and they can be more efficiently utilized by anyone who is interested in understanding and exploring the essential nature of Adler's system.

1. *We are more alike than different* Perhaps one of the most essential underlying examples in all of this is that, though we all behave uniquely, we are all still more alike than different.

2. *Cooperation: a biological necessity* Because human beings are the weakest and slowest to develop among all living organisms, cooperation is a biological necessity, not just a social one. This is the "iron law of co-living," as Adler called it. Though man in his technological and intellectual development has evolved to the point that some individuals apparently can ignore this law with relative impunity, even in this competitive world, cooperation is still absolute. In most cities, if the trucks and trains were to stop bringing food to its inhabitants, most of them would starve in weeks, or, if the water faucets were turned off, die in hours. This principle is only most noticeable in times of crisis, but the degree to which a person willingly cooperates with others still determines how successful his relationships with others are.

3. *All behavior is purposive* There are no random acts nor senseless crimes. All our attitudes, feelings, and actions are aimed toward an holistic and unifying goal, which Adler called "fictive" because it is an abstraction, and its true motive is hidden from consciousness. Actions that are not in conflict with the goal can be casual and have the appearance of randomness, but any response to outside stimuli is screened in advance by this unifying force before the individual acts on it and will only behave in accordance with it.

4. *Behavior is based on our perception of reality, not necessarily reality itself* That which we perceive as real is acted upon accordingly, whether others see it similarly or not. Most aberrations of behavior that may be otherwise diagnosed as neurotic, criminal, or even psychotic, are the result of mistaken perceptions, usually about those around us, and cannot be attributed to "instinctual" forces.

5. *The need to belong is fundamental to human nature* Other than the essential requirements for life (i.e., air, water, food, and adequate shelter), the primary need of every human being is affection. If the growing child lacks this, he will substitute approval or attention, however negative it might be, for the love he feels has been denied him. In an adult this need usually translates into the need to belong to a group, family, or community.

6. *We believe in accordance with what we want, not what we are* Adler called his system "the psychology of use, not posession." All Adlerian practitioners look for a goal behind a given behavior rather than a label like *obsessive–compulsive* or *attention deficit disorder*.

7. *All human beings are equal* Despite many varying capacities, all of us are equal as human beings. Adler recognized very early, however, that males and females compete for status in all societies that consider masculine values superior to feminine. He called this tendency, which is still overwhelmingly prevalent today, "masculine protest."

8. *We are all responsible for our acts* Regardless of motivation, we are all responsible for (though not necessarily guilty of) our own acts. The same is true of our attitudes toward others. No one can be truly free without being responsible as well.

9. *We all have a potential for social interest* Adler believed that every person has, his own "innate predisposition" for social interest, which he called *Gemeinschafts-gefühl*, and which is roughly equivalent to Abraham Maslow's *self-actualization*. However, this potential must be nurtured in order to be fully realized.

10. *All our attitudes are learned* We are not born with genetically predisposed attitudes. We may have physical infirmities that strongly influence our developing attitudes, but the attitudes themselves are learned and therefore can be unlearned. Proper care and nurturing of an infant can help to overcome even very severe physical handicaps.

11. *We compensate for alleged as well as real inferiorites* Every person compensates, both physiologically and psychologically, for any handicap, whether it is an actual inferiority or a perceived one, such as being too short, too tall, or not bright enough. Any significant difference in a person's appearance or behavior can result in overcompensation.

12. *Consciousness and unconsciousness are merely levels of awareness* Although the conscious mind ultimately rules, actually most of our basic bodily as well as psychological functions are mediated by the brain outside of our awareness. These functions range from driving a car, to playing the piano, to the circulation of the blood. The former operate at the subconscious or peripheral level, of which we are somewhat but not fully aware. The latter operate without our knowledge unless some interference to the process occurs.

13. *The cure is reeducation* The process of curing or eliminating a person's neurotic or psychotic problem is essentially one of unlearning mistaken perceptions. However, in the case of psychotics, the use of certain medication can bring the person back into awareness of reality so that he can be helped. In therapy, the therapist aids the client in discovering his mistaken social perceptions and helps him to change them. Behavioral problems in children are much more amenable to change than those in adults. Both Adler and Dreikurs successfully promoted widescale programs in schools to try to change aberrant behavior in children.

The following chapters are devoted to an in-depth explanation of these concepts, as well as descriptions of some of the methods Adlerians have and are using to implement his ideas in working not only with adults, but more important with teachers, children, and parents.

The final chapter in this book is this writer's attempt to analyze the present state of the world from an Adlerian perspective. Because these issues are primarily political, solutions perhaps unfortunately are also in the hands of the politicians. How we can influence them to look at these immense problems from a more Adlerian perspective is only one question to which ours and later generations will have to address themselves.

Chapter Two

Inferiority Feelings
and the Fictive Goal

It seems somewhat ironic that although the concepts of inferiority feelings and the fictive goal are integral parts of Adlerian theory, they may be the least known of Adler's ideas today. Since the 1956 publication of *The Individual Psychology of Alfred Adler* by the Ansbachers [18] (the first definitive work on Adlerian theory since Wexberg [76]) most of the modern practicians, and particularly those under the influence of Dreikurs, have tended to concentrate more of what has been labeled "growth motivation" in dealing with maladaptive behavior. Interestingly enough, what was known as the "inferiority complex," which grew out of Adler's formulations concerning the nature of what he called "normal" feelings of inferiority, became surprisingly popular in this country, not only among psychologists and psychiatrists, but lay people as well during the late 1920s and 1930s. However, the concept was somewhat deemphasized in his later writings and has been almost entirely discarded by modern Adlerians. This was probably done to avoid the negative impact that the notion of "inferiority feelings" and the "inferiority complex" had created among the public during those years. Being an abstraction, the concept of the fictive goal was also somewhat sidestepped by later Adlerians in favor of the more concrete "lifestyle" as the basis of personality.

THE NATURE OF INFERIORITY FEELINGS

Often the death of an idea comes about as much because it has either an unpopular connotation or because it is mistakenly interpreted. Though few of us like the idea of being considered inferior to anything (or in particular, to anyone else), many of us still consider ourselves inferior to others and often may use these feelings in a neurotic fashion to keep us from trying new challenges or taking risks.

Why Inferiority Feelings?

Adler's early followers tended to take his word virtually as gospel and were apt to ask what and how, but rarely why. Yet, it is only when one asks why do we begin to understand what Adler called "normal" feelings of inferiority to reach an imaginary goal of "near god likeness," as he sometimes described it. Retracing the steps that led Adler to this conclusion makes the process clearer.

Adler's first significant discovery in this direction was contained in a monograph entitled *Organ Inferiority and Its Psychological Compensation* [1] first published in 1907. He proposed that compensation for biological inferiority is not only physiological, but essentially psychological in nature as well. He believed all our behavior is essentially holistic, and not only do our physical organs attempt to compensate for deficiencies or loss through accident or illness, *but so do our psychological mechanisms*. Some of this has been suggested, at least later in physiological studies, particularly by Walter B. Cannon in his *Wisdom of the Body* [23] and Hans Selye in *The Stress of Life* [62]. Cannon coined the term "homeostasis" to describe what he saw as a process of "leveling up," or attempting to develop a continuous state of physiological equilibrium in the body's functioning. In this process, should for example a sugar deficiency develop, the body will manufacture certain enzymes that attempt to correct this disequilibrium. In extreme cases the person may experience a craving for sweets until the deficiency is overcome. One of Adler's greatest contributions to our knowledge of personality may have been his suggestion that our psychological mechanisms appear to operate in a similar fashion. Adler also described a process which he labeled "overcompensation." For example, if a kidney is lost or removed, the remaining kidney often functions more efficiently than the previous two did, because the "lazier" organ often tended to "pull back" or slow the operation of the other, more efficient kidney.

In his description of the process of physiological shock, Selye described it as a mechanism by which the body attempts to compensate or overcompensate for a very severe, sudden injury or illness. Often, this compensation is so exaggerated that the shock itself may be fatal, even though the injury or illness might not itself have caused death. This would seem to suggest that psychical overcompensation, as Adler called it, is also a biological process and operates according to somewhat the same principles as described by both Cannon and Selye.

The Overcompensation of Genius

Some years ago I was reminded rather sharply by R. Rowena Ansbacher that Adler had *never* stated that "genius is compensation for an inferior brain." I now remember that this quote came from Lydia Sicher, from whom I learned much of my original Adlerian theory. Although there is no way of knowing whether this was an idea Adler seriously supported, any statement so startling, if this did indeed come from Adler, deserves attention. Though he did once say that "for almost all out-standing people, we find some organ imperfection," apparently the quote Sicher attributed to him was never found in Adler's writings. One might presume he might have meant compensation for an "allegedly" inferior brain, rather than one of actual physical deformity, perhaps by an individual who has been told by teachers or parents that he had inferior mental ability. An example of this could be found in Albert Einstein, who reportedly was thought by some of his teachers to have been stupid because he failed mathematics in school. We all know that he went on to become one of the supreme mathematical geniuses of all time. It would be presumptuous to assume that Einstein's brilliant achievements came about as a result of that one failure, but it could have been part of a sequence of frustrations that led to his extraordinary later development.

However, in view of the obvious controversy that was generated by some of Adler's statements about the compensatory behavior of genius, Adler did issue a caution as to the way this concept should be interpreted. He said, "Many persons have resented the attention that I and my colleagues have drawn to the compensatory factor in the work of artists of genius or of high talent and have attempted to deny that which our experience is constantly confirming. But their objection is due to a misunderstanding of the findings of individual psychology. We are not so foolish as to suppose that organic imperfection is the efficient cause of genius." This does suggest that he might have at one time made the statement to which Sicher refers:

Many Freudians have indeed supposed that the sublime works of human genius were directly caused by sexual repressions, but we make no such eccentric generalization.

In our view, a man of genius is primarily a man of supreme usefulness. If he is an artist he is useful to culture, giving distinction and value by his work to the recreative life of many thousands. This value, where it is genuine and not merely empty brilliance, depends upon a high degree of courage and social interest. The origin of genius lies neither in the inherited organism nor in the environmental influences, but in that third sphere of individual reaction which also includes socially affirmative action. In the choice of its specialized expression, however, the highest talent is conditioned by the organism with which it is endowed, from the greatest defect of which it gains its particular mode of concentration.

If we apply the social measure to artists and poets, we note that they serve a social function more than anyone else. It is they who have taught us how to see, to hear, to think, and how to feel. We owe them the greatest good of mankind. Thus, we attribute to them the greatest dignity, that of being the friends and leaders of mankind.

Genius is to be defined as no more than supreme usefulness; it is only when a man's life is recognized by others as having significance for them that we call him a genius. The meaning expressed in such a life will always be, "Life means—to contribute to the whole." We are not speaking here of professed motives. We are closing our ears to professions and looking at achievements.

Mankind only calls those individuals geniuses who have contributed much to the common welfare. We cannot imagine a genius who has left no advantage to mankind behind him. [18, p. 153]

Here he suggests that though the initial stimulus might have originated from an organ deficiency, many other factors, cultural as well as personal, have led to the development of genius. It should also be emphasized that for the tiny number of individuals who overcame a physical handicap to achieve greatness, there were millions with other similar handicaps who unfortunately did not.

Experiments with individuals who have suffered strokes or brain tumors, or had surgery as a result of epilepsy, do indicate that the brain, as do all bodily organs, compensates for physical defects, sometimes to an outstanding degree. Because it is now known that the two hemispheres of the brain have very different functions, the loss of one half (which has never been evaluated because no person has survived the full loss of one half of his brain), would not appear to result in the remaining hemisphere taking up slack, so to speak, for the lack of function of the other.

However, a rather startling review of the brain functioning of three hydrocephalic adults was the subject of a recent research study described on television. By a new process of brain scanning, the researchers were able to isolate those areas of the cortex that were functioning electrically against those which were not. In all the cases the brain scans revealed that these individuals functioned at an extraordinarily high intellectual level, utilizing only a small portion of the cortex usually considered necessary for normal functioning. The rest of the brain in these scans did not appear to be generating any electrical energy at all. One person was a mathematical genius and the others were performing at a level far superior to even most college graduates.

So, what might have appeared to have been a generalization which Adler himself later attempted to "explain" away could possibly be a far more profound insight than even he imagined. More investigation of this nature needs to be done to ascertain just how important this statement may be.

We are familiar with similar examples of what Adler described as psychical overcompensation for organ inferiorities in other capacities, such as Beethoven's having written his Ninth Symphony when he was totally deaf; the Greek Demosthenes, a stutterer who became a great orator; and the dwarf, Toulouse Lautrec, who was an extraordinary genius as an artist. Perhaps even the degree of statesmanship and self-actualization achieved by Roosevelt in his later years—as Maslow has suggested—might be partially attributed to an attack of polio which left him crippled at the age of thirty. Of course, the question always remains as to whether these individuals would have made as great a contribution without the presence of the inferiority or not. Perhaps the next step that Adler took may in itself furnish more clues to answer this question.

Compensation for Alleged Inferiorities

Adler's next most significant insight beyond his theory of organ inferiority was in his realization that compensation and overcompensation may occur as readily as the result of alleged inferiorities, as well as real ones. This can take both negative and positive forms.

Inferiority Feelings Are Comparative.   Following the context of Adler's original formulations on organ inferiority, this would mean that although the individual might not have a physical defect in a particular area in which he is concerned, if he *considers* himself inferior in this capacity to others, his psychical and even physiological compensation would be similar, as if he possessed a genuine organ inferiority. In order to actually feel inferior to anyone else for any reason, it would appear that a human would have to make a comparison between himself regarding the particular defect—alleged or real—with someone else and find himself lacking. When one stands out in the desert or on a mountaintop on a cloudless night, one may feel small and insignificant in comparison to the grandeur and scope he sees. However it would seem unlikely that he would consider this in terms of possessing an inferiority, generally because the term "inferiority" denotes being "less than" something it could be the equal of. The concept of inferiority would not seem to develop until the child, at a particular stage in his early development, realizes he is somehow like these huge creatures who surround him and who seem to be able to do everything perfectly, including satisfying his desires as well as their own needs. Thus, feelings of inferiority would seem to be almost entirely *comparative*—although contemplating our own mortality has generated assumptions about our inadequacies in most of us at one time or another. Even there, the comparative process takes place. When we die, we apparently cease to function at this level while others go on. When we become old we often liken ourselves—usually more unfavorably than not—to the young, who seem at the moment to function with such freedom and ease, almost to be able to live forever. While at the same time, the very young consider themselves inferior to those who are older! When we are ill we compare ourselves unfavorably to those who are well and often use this as a means to gain attention and service from others. Inferiority feelings very often arise as a result of these comparisons, whether we consider them normal or not.

Adler was quick to realize that the human race was far more bedeviled by alleged inferiorities than by real ones. Being too tall or too short, of a different color or race than others, not pretty enough, strong enough, or athletic enough—all are means by which people see themselves as inferior to each other.

How Inferior Are We?   It is true that everyone individually is probably always constitutionally or even intellectually inferior to someone else in one way or another. Yet, all too often how we *regard* ourselves with respect to our peers often seems to have little basis in fact at all. In a society where intellectual capacity is generally more a measure of a person's success than any other trait, the excessively short person still overcompensates intellectually in ways which may be beneficial, but perhaps more often or not. Alexander the Great and Napoleon may be said to be examples of this. Simply, to them being physically smaller than others appeared to mean being inferior; consequently becoming military leaders and exercising enormous power over nearly the whole world during their times may have been to them a major means of overcoming their attitudes about their inferiority of stature. The behavior of those around a particular individual may also contribute greatly in enhancing feelings of alleged inferiority. It was not long ago when a six-foot woman was deemed to be a freak and viewed as an object of pity or derision. In the days of Rembrandt, obesity was considered a sign of beauty (probably because the few overweight people were usually the only ones who had enough to eat, and were consequently envied by those who did not). Today, the excessively obese person is considered to be "different" and usually more deficient because of this trait.

The Inferiority Complex.   Adler also commenced using the term "inferiority complex" to describe those people who, for whatever reason, were unable to compensate for their feelings of inferiority in a positive and cooperative manner.

The inferiority (symptom) complex describes the attitude of an individual who by this complex expresses that he is not in the position to solve an existing problem. It must not be confused with the normal inferiority feelings. The inferiority (symptom) complex is the representation of the person to himself and others that he is not strong enough to solve a given problem in a socially useful way. Needless to say, no point of rest is given in this way. The total mood with all its thought, feeling, and action material is pointed toward failure. [18, p. 169]

In Adler's view, the development of the so-called inferiority complex would lead to an exaggerated striving for superiority which he labeled the "superiority complex."

If a person is a show-off it is only because he feels inferior, because he does not feel strong enough to compete with others on the useful side of life. That is why he stays on the useless side. He is not in harmony with society. It seems to be a trait of human nature that when individuals—both children and adults—feel weak, they cease to be interested socially, but strive for (personal) superiority. [18, p. 260]

THE NECESSITY OF FICTIONS

Adler's formulations on the assumption of "fictions" has been one of his most important but neglected contributions to our knowledge of human behavior and thought. He acknowledged that many of the ideas underlying this concept came from the German philosopher, Hans Vaihinger, whose philosophy of "as if" first appeared in published form in 1911, the year Adler withdrew from Freud's circle. Vaihinger proposed that if we perceive something as real, we will then act "as if" it were so and behave accordingly. He also suggested that the idea of fictions or conscious and unconscious ideas that have no counterpart in reality, can often enable us to deal with reality more effectively than we could otherwise. Adler expanded Vaihinger's thesis into a concept he called "tendentious apperception" (later called "biased apperception" by Dreikurs), which helped lay the foundation of what we now call the "phenomenological" approach to behavior. It may be surprising to the average adult to realize how many fictions he may use in the course of a single day to help him move through life. This comes about because we are seldom in possession of *all* the information about any given subject at any given time, but we are constantly forced to make decisions as to how to proceed with this inadequate knowledge. Therefore, we make certain assumptions, part of which may be based on these fictions, to organize our environment to help us move along this path. A brilliant example suggested by Adler in 1912 is one of the most useful fictions utilized by the navigator on a ship or plane in the middle of the ocean. By imagining fictitious lines cutting across the globe which we call meridians and parallels, and forming squares of them which are drawn on a map, such lines can then be projected out into space into what is called the "celestial sphere." By the utilization of time, which is also another fiction in our existence, if either the stars or sun are visible, we can compute where any particular square will be with relationship to either the position of the sun or stars at any given moment, by measuring with a sextant the angle of the sun or a given star relative to the horizon. A series of tables then tells the navigator where the ship is in relation to the sun or stars at that particular time. With this celestial surveyor, he can then quite accurately find his position on the surface of the ocean.

Of course, psychologically normal and reasonably intelligent adults can reach consensus fairly easily, at least with respect to objective phenomena such as material things, whether they are useful or not. But in the area which is least objective, that of human relationships, often much of our belief about the attitudes of others toward us may be fictional but is still treated as real and we react accordingly. We may consider such fictions to be useful to us, but often if antisocial, they may do us far more harm than good. To the small child, his limited experience and understanding of what he sees causes him to interpret in fictional terms. A desk becomes a tunnel to play under, or, if he bangs his head on an object that hurts him, it is to be avoided. These experiences and the child's interpretation of them help to eventually form his concept of what Adler suggested it would be like to live in a world where all of his problems were solved. Not all fictions, of course, are useful. His belief in the fiction that all adults are godlike can give him problems later in particular if these adults are abusive or cold toward him.

Movement in Behavior

Because all our behavior consists in moving toward a direction or goal, or from a "minus to a plus situation," as Adler described it, this imagined state or objective becomes expressed as a superlative: to be the strongest, the best, the greatest, the worst. Even its more concrete manifestations in the choice of occupations are themselves grandiose and fictional. One classic example described by Adler is of one little boy who he was counseling. The boy was asked what he would like to be when he grew up. He replied that he wanted to be a motorman (streetcar conductor). When Adler asked him why, the child's response was, "So that I can take the people where *I* want them to go." From this can be assumed the beginning of a goal of control over others, but it also represents the fiction that the child's inadequate understanding led him to believe. He sees himself and others sitting in the back of the car and sees the conductor operating the controls and the car moving here and there, with people getting on and off at various places. The child has no awareness that the car only goes where the tracks lead it and that the conductor only takes it where those for whom he works want it to go. Again, this would seem to represent an example of what Piaget has observed in children's monologues where they fantasize moving objects which they cannot do in reality.

Another child of whom Adler asked the same question, replied, "I want to be a grave digger." When asked why, the boy replied, "So I can bury all the rest."

Formalizing the Goal

Though much of this has to be considered speculative, it may be possible that the fictive goal only becomes formalized when we reach the stage of what one might call "self-awareness" regarding self-consciousness or *being aware that one is aware*. Perhaps the most important fiction of all in this developmental process is the concept of time, which is our way of measuring movement. At least as far as our individual perceptions are concerned, there appears only to be the *present*. But at the same time this "present" is constantly moving ahead into what we call the "future." Lydia Sicher referred to this process as "duration." We recall the past only as memories of what has happened or what we have read or heard about, even though we may associate elements of it with what we are experiencing in the present. The future is only something we can predict, but because we tend not to conceptualize the present as movement, we often tend to view past and future as "entities" rather than fictions. Because we have the ability to predict, we also want to be prepared for any and all eventualities which might arise, and according to Adler, we organize all of these assumptions into what we call the "fictive final goal." He called this goal "teleological" because it was always future oriented but still firmly rooted in our biological origin, rather than having a spiritual or religious origin.

THE WILL TO POWER

During his theorizing about the effects or attempts to psychologically overcome inferiority feelings, Adler made an interpretation previously described, which he later saw as incorrect. In the early development of his theoretical system he had suggested that our attempts to overcome even our normal feelings of inferiority led us to try and reach a position of superiority over others, which he called the "will to power." Because of the prevailing opinion of society in those days, that the male was superior to the female, this was further defined to mean *masculine* superiority. What was then evoked was the male ideal—strong, intelligent, logical, powerful—as opposed to the female model, which was weak, intuitive, impressionable, and indecisive. Though Adler correctly saw that this masculine ego ideal was a fiction, he still believed that the fundamental goal of both sexes was to reach this goal of so-called "masculine" superiority over others. At the time, he called this drive the "masculine protest."

Love Instead of Power

When Adler returned to his friends and coworkers from his service in the Austrian Army, and they began again the brilliant, often heated discussions in the coffee houses of Vienna, he announced that he had decided the basic human motivation was social interest and not power as he had previously asserted. His followers were astounded. Some were even outraged, and it was a considerable time before they began to truly comprehend the profound implications behind Adler's dramatic change in attitude. Though he still considered the drive prevalent among both sexes was to attain a goal of masculine superiority, he now saw this as a mistaken objective, and therefore a neurotic one. Social interest—the correct goal—could only be cooperative and arose from the need for love and affection (later defined by Dreikurs as the need to "belong") present in all of us. What Adler later defined as social interest was what he saw as an innate potentiality within all of us, but one that of necessity could only be developed by learning how to cooperate freely and willingly with others. Much of the implications of this concept today have been neglected. We will explore them, particularly as they relate to present day male/female relationships, in a later chapter.

The Striving for Significance

In his later writings, Adler relabeled this fundamental inner drive as a "striving for significance," which meant that one could only consider himself worthwhile and adequate if he felt that he was significant in the eyes of others. For all too many people, even today, the hidden booby trap in this statement is no matter how adequate others actually see us as being, what we believe about our own self-worth is the true criterion of our own feelings of adequacy.

Lydia Sicher offered some clarification to this objective on more pragmatic grounds by suggesting that our drives could be either "horizontal" in cooperating with others in solving mutual problems, or "vertical," where the individual was presumed to be on a fictitious ladder with others either a rung below or above him. To achieve vertical status one must step over someone else to move "up" the ladder. According to Sicher, going from a "minus" to a "plus" in fulfilling a goal in a vertical direction would be neurotic, whereas in fulfilling the horizontal goal of achieving a "plus" situation, the impetus comes from one's enhanced feelings of self-worth when willingly cooperating with others to make life easier and more satisfying for everyone [65].

INFERIORITY FEELINGS AT BIRTH

Perhaps to conceptualize this in another way would be to describe the process of personality development as follows: As infants we are born almost totally helpless and indeed are inferior to nearly every living thing around us. But as we are also born with a tremendous instinctual drive to overcome this frustrating situation, which ultimately translates itself into a need to control those factors over which we, at birth, have little or no dominance. As we become older we begin to discover that somehow these needs are at least momentarily satisfied by these huge creatures around us who appear to resemble us. Our first desire is to be as much like them as possible, until we discover, which we inevitably do, that they are powerful but not omnipotent. When we become old enough to realize that we are not part of them, but are separate entities, we begin to compare ourselves with them as to whether we are inferior or superior in whatever characteristics in which we feel similar to them. From this comes what Adler referred to as the goal of "god likeness"—of being not only equal to others but superior to *all* individuals or forces which we encounter. According to Adler, the balance of our life consists of attempting to reconcile the demands of our environment to this lofty goal we have set for ourselves. The degree to which we are able to achieve this compromise largely determines the ultimate amount of satisfaction we derive from living.

Whether the goal is a single, unifying force that we follow blindly throughout our lives or whether it is a series of precepts that we form into a pattern, may never be known. But many psychologists will now agree that we set up internally and externally what Adler called a "style of life," which is a set of attitudes and behaviors that we develop as we move through life. Though the behaviors themselves may change, the underlying precepts rarely do, and we must all learn one way or another the harsh fact that we can never completely control our environment. In general, those who learn to work with others in a communal effort to control the problems we encounter achieve a much greater measure of self-satisfaction than those who attempt to achieve superiority over others.

The Process of Growth

In an effort to clarify this it seems important to delineate some of the more significant alterations in the child's intellectual and personality development that occur in the early years, some of which appear to correlate significantly with the experiments and theories described by other more recent cognitive theorists, particularly the Swiss psychologist, Jean Piaget. Although Adler specifically never formulated an age level at which this appeared, he talked at length about the child's conceptualization of what he believed the adults about him were like. He called this the "prototype," which emerges as not necessarily a single person such as a father or mother, another adult, or an older child, but as a conglomerate or state of "grown-upness," attributing to others qualities which in the child's imagination usually far exceed the capacities that any adult would possess.

Separateness: the First Landmark Change

Somewhere between the ages of two and four years, the child appears to become aware that he is separate from others and no longer part of his mother—or of all those around him—as he previously surmised. At least two examples from my own experience can perhaps be presented to illustrate this. The first was with our own daughter, who at age two was shown a picture of the five of us in the family. She identified her mother, myself, the oldest, and middle girl, but she did not identify herself. She was not aware of who she was at that moment. A year later when we showed her the same picture she said, "That's me!" Another interesting example occurred in a family during one of my counseling sessions with a mother who had identical twin boys. At the time of the occurrence they were two years old. When she asked the boy, Mike, as he was looking in the mirror, who he saw, he would respond, "That's Matt," his twin brother. Matt would correspondingly call the vision in the mirror, Mike. About a year later they were somewhat able to identify themselves as being the image in the mirror rather than the twin. A further possible verification of this developmental phase would appear to be in the phenomenon of the "parallel play" versus "social play," which has been observed by many child development researchers in recent years. Until the ages of two to four, most children will play individually alongside other children without seeming to be aware of each other. Social play, representing interaction between them, suggests that they have become aware of their "separateness" when they move into this phase of their development.

The Theories of Piaget

According to the French psychologist, Jean Piaget [59], at about age two the child begins to develop into what he terms the "semiotic stage," where he is beginning to make something—a mental symbol, a word or object—stand for or represent something else which it is not. For example, the child at that age can use a mental picture of a ball to stand in for a real ball that is not in view at the moment. A child can also imitate the temper tantrum of another child after he has observed it because he can visualize this as a mental "image" of what happened. Though Piaget did not specifically refer to the idea of "separateness" between child and others, it would seem that the ability to substitute a mental symbol for the real thing would be the first step in the child's becoming aware that he is "different" from others, as well as from the objects with which he plays. At first he may only imitate another child's behavior, but the mental symbol ultimately would seem to furnish a concept of others as being representations of himself, yet different, and as a result, separate.

It would also appear that the ability to substitute a mental symbol for an object would appear to be the first step in abstract thought. Imitation, which at first only takes place immediately following another's action, becomes internalized and ultimately takes place without the object being present.

Four to Seven Years

During this period according to Piaget, the most important growth in the child's intellectual function is the development and use of language. Though much of the child's world during this period is ego centered and involves repetitive copying of another child's speech without responding to it, he described two modes of language which occurred at about this age: "individual monologue," where the child sits down and talks out loud about what he wants to do; and "collective monologue," which represents a child talking when others are around, but does not seem to pay attention to what he is saying. However, after age four, more than half a child's speech now involves communicating with others—this then is the first genuine attempt at socialization. This also may be the beginning of comparisons. Though in communicative speech the child begins to transmit information, or repetition of what another child says or does, he seems unable to justify his own opinions or to recognize contrary opinions as different from his. Piaget suggests the child uses individual fantasies to express a type of wish fulfillment. If he would like to move a box that is too heavy, he may *tell* the box to move, thus using words to accomplish what he cannot do himself. Here could possibly be the beginnings of formulation of a goal of how things would be if the *particular problem at hand were solved*. The child's fantasies themselves also serve as vehicles for such goal striving.

Though the child at this age is beginning to realize that others behave and act differently from himself, it would seem possible to infer from Piaget's findings that his behavior and concepts are totally involved in finding a satisfactory way of dealing with the world from his own self-interest. Such things as cooperation and social interest are simply not understood in his limited perception of reality at this state. Consequently, most of his attempts are directed toward meeting and coping with the puzzling and often frustrating experiences with which he is dealing.

FORMALIZING THE GOAL

Ansbacher suggests that when the individual reaches self-consciousness he is immediately confronted with challenges to his goal. Because he has already trained himself to make interpretations of what he sees at a subconscious or preconscious level, what he sees in his environment will be rejected if it does not fit the goal because he is not consciously aware that a better way would be possible. For example, if his goal is that of the pampered child who wants to be served, he still will see those experiences where service is denied him as being the fault of the denier rather than his own. Rather than accepting the fact that he must cooperate in order to receive positive attention from others, he lends his efforts to finding those who will serve him by becoming passive and nonfunctioning or by indulging in temper tantrums when he does not get his way. He also learns that this is a form of recognition that, though not the best kind, is at least better than rejection. Consequently, even punishments and failures may not deter him from attempting to reach this goal. Only by being *shown* that he can attain satisfaction by being more cooperative can he be induced to change his behavior.

ADDED COMPARISONS WITH PIAGET

Because Piaget developed most of his theories about cognitive behavior development in terms of the child's dealing with objects rather than in interactions with others, only a few inferences may be drawn from his later studies on what he calls "classification." Piaget considered the child's having reached a change in cognitive development at age seven or eight in terms of how he learns to classify objects.

For example, if a series of blocks have different sizes, this represents one classification in which one differentiates them in size. Then if they are also colored differently, this represents a second classification, namely color. A third would be shape. Piaget's experiments with children between seven and eight showed they were sometimes able to see similarity between objects, yet they could not grasp the concept of class. In one experiment, children were given little toys that represented people, objects, and animals. When asked for all objects like a horse, one child gave the questioner all the animals and then a baby and two trees. In Piaget's experiments, most children age seven and older seemed to be able to think simultaneously in terms of wholes and parts. The child can understand the relationships between objects he sees but still does not seem to be able to do the same thing when imagining classes involved. This stage, Piaget called "concrete operational."

In terms of relating this to the fictive goal, it would appear that the child has learned to generalize and differentiate between objects (and as well, behavior of others toward him). He can then conceptualize a series of responses to his experience but still is unable to render them into specific abstractions. Possibly the utilization of the unifying concept of a goal as Adler has suggested may be the result of the child's inability to discriminate between responses to the problems he faces intellectually. He may then lump them all into *one* class represented by being the best, the strongest, or the smartest, and then attempts to use his one concept to help him interpret all of his day-to-day problems. By the time he reaches the final stage in Piaget's developmental scheme, where he can manipulate imaginary concepts in his mind, he has already learned to interpret stimuli in terms of the simplistic, more concrete type of goal he has learned at age seven or earlier. Consequently, though his cognitive level has improved, he still interprets even through the screen he has set up, because it has become an automatic process below the level of awareness.

THE POSSIBILITY OF CHANGE

Perhaps one very important aspect of Adler's thinking does need to be emphasized. He felt that because the goal was *learned* it could, in effect, be unlearned. Essentially he and all of his followers view counseling and psychotherapy as a process of reeducation. Adler rejected the Freudian notion of basic instinctual drives of a destructive nature, and even went so far as to suggest that nearly anyone could change their goal, or at least their basic behavior if they wanted to badly enough. This, at the time he stated it in the early 1920s, was far more revolutionary and challenging than is realized today. It does suggest hope for humanity, not in attempting to suppress instinctual forces beyond their control, but by developing insight into mistaken perceptions about others that can be corrected.

In developing his system, Adler also emphasized a principle which the Ansbachers have attributed to William James, that of "soft determinism" as contrasted to the "hard determinism" which are instinctual behavior responses to stimuli suggested by Freud and his followers [18, p. 5]. According to Adler, we ourselves still decide on a goal, but once we formulate it, we are in effect "determined" by it. However, if the goal is faulty, it can be changed through a process of psychotherapy.

THE BEHAVIORISTS

Although Freud's views appeared to vary considerably from those of the behaviorists, essentially all of them considered human behavior to be a "result" of more or less predetermined or built-in responses to what happened to individuals in the environment. Determinism suggests that human functioning, though admittedly somewhat more complex than that of lower animals, operates along the same lines. However, though it is true that the first response of a person would be to yank his hand away from a painful electric shock, as would any animal try to avoid such punishment, a person *can* leave his hand there if he chooses. Although the behaviorists might fashion an elaborate theoretical description as to how he has become conditioned to not respond the way he is supposed to, the fact is that he may make many such choices where most animals, responding to their instinctual drives, will not. Such a choice is the result of a person's interpretation of the situation, a phenomenon which the behaviorists have never adequately explained, or perhaps even understand.

THE PHENOMENON OF INSIGHT

Wolfgang Kohler's [47] experiments with the great apes at the Canary Islands during World War I would perhaps be another example that appears to reinforce Adler's concept, but is inadequately explained by the behaviorists. In Kohler's experiments his most intelligent ape, Sultan, was put in a cage with a series of boxes and a banana hanging from a rope at the top. In the beginning Sultan kept charging around trying to reach the banana unsuccessfully by climbing the bars and boxes or jumping as well as rolling the boxes. Then he suddenly experienced what Kohler describes as a "flash" of insight. Sultan immediately piled one box on top of another, climbed up, and claimed the banana. Two years later, when confronted with the same problem, the ape immediately repeated the process, which indicated that what had gone on in his mind was a permanent insight, or an actual remembered experience that cannot be explained by conditioning or extinction, as the behaviorists interpret it.

There have been numerous studies verifying this process of insight in human subjects, though it appears not to be present in the behavior of most animals on a lower intellectual scale than apes.

ALTERING THE GOAL

A philosophical question among Adlerians that seems to have never been entirely resolved as yet has been whether those who support the concept of a fictive goal or even that of the lifestyle believe that as a result of successful efforts to change, the individual actually alters his goal or merely readapts it to a new situation that is less frustrating but may still achieve similar results. For example, if a person has a goal of superiority over others, but is clever and versatile, he may end up in a management position where he has many people serving him. He can then use this method for reinforcing rather than changing the goal.

Adler himself, as well as Sicher and many other Adlerians, contended the goal itself could only be altered through therapy or possibly through an intense personal revelation, during which the person achieves enough insight into the mistaken nature of his goal to change it. Possible examples of this suggested by Sicher were Buddha and Leo Tolstoy, the Russian novelist, both of whom in their middle years abruptly abandoned a life of relative ease and material abundance to travel among and serve the poor.

IS THERE A GOAL?

Again, though there never can be any ultimate verification whether a single final goal exists within human beings or is merely a system of interconnected objectives and attitudes, there is growing evidence that we do appear to operate as an holistic unit, with all our behavior being relevant and purposive—at least to us—and that our basic personalities remain remarkably consistent, even though our behavior may change dramatically. This would certainly attest to the possibility of a governing principle behind behavior. Only when we are led to the point where our mistaken perceptions lead us to such misery and frustration, that our existence becomes intolerable, do we take one of two courses. We either retreat from the real world, as does the psychotic, and pretend we have achieved the goal, or we seek help. Perhaps there is a third alternative, as Adler has described it, in the rapidly growing criminal mentality, where we embark upon a revengeful crusade in an attempt to retaliate for the world's having refused to accept our goal as we see it.

THE GOAL OF GENIUS: THE FOURTH ALTERNATIVE?

Another, most fascinating speculation about the possibility of a single unified individual goal was Lydia Sicher's suggestion regarding the difference between the goal of a creative genius and that of others. To her, the goal of the genius was in his *work, and everything else in his life was subordinate*.

When one sees the extraordinary perseverance and single-minded effort that seems characteristic of most creative geniuses, perhaps the realism of the goal may be a little more apparent. Perhaps the genius comes closer to realizing his goal than anyone and yet we can see it as a single, enormously compelling, unifying drive that impels him to sacrifice nearly everything else in its pursuit. To Adler, the goal of every individual is just as compelling, but its manifestations are much less visible. Often they are never seen clearly except when the person is in a crisis situation. The genius, on the other hand seems almost in a perpetual crisis, and one may see in his behavior the unifying processes that are present in all of us. As Adler has repeatedly suggested, perhaps we could utilize these creative forces that are in each of us as the genius does if we could only become aware of how to do it.

Further insight to this puzzling phenomena may be contained in a fascinating article which came to light a few years ago, "A Preface to the Diary of Vaslav Nijinsky" [17], written by Adler and published for the first time with a detailed discussion by Heinz Ansbacher. Vaslav Nijinsky (1888–1950), considered by many to be the greatest ballet dancer of all time, became psychotic in 1919 and was confined to a sanitorium. Adler visited him in 1934, as had a number of the most eminent specialists of the day in mental disorders, including Freud, Jung, Bleuler, Kraepelin, and Ferenezci. Adler apparently was the only one of them to write about his visit and this preface was released in 1978, by her request only after Nijinsky's widow died. In it, Adler suggests how the "god likeness" or unachievable need for perfection implied in Nijinsky's goal may have led him to his great heights of achievement and physical prowess but then betrayed him in the end.

The difficulty encountered by laymen and psychiatrists, as I can see it, is that they always measure with their own idea of vanity, of castles in the air, and of appreciation. But this is a hundred and hundred times surpassed by the passion which flares in the minds of the neurotic and psychotic. Their exuberance of vanity, full of expectations of elevation, brings about automatically the shock effects and the retreat from social life. There is no "split" in their personality.

Whoever can see the life of a schizophrenic in the coherence, as I tried to explain, will admit it: *if the conception of life of a schizophrenic person were right, if really the meaning of life were godlikeness, then the choice of schizophrenia would be the best possible choice—because it resembles death.* And the problem of death always occurs when a person feels, rightly or wrongly, that he is cut off from successful achievement in his individual striving. [17, p. 134]

Adler also discussed the "purpose" of irrationality as he saw it reflected in Nijinsky's behavior:

The schizophrenic patient is the purest advocate of irrationality. There is a great temptation among men, even among philosophers down to our times, to disregard what binds us all—namely, the highest development of common sense, which nobody can contradict—and instead, driven by what I have called an "inferiority complex," to soar and to indulge in their otherwise frustrated vanity.

Nijinsky's way goes in this direction. He detests "thinking"; nobody is right who thinks. You must feel. Our poor hero, badly prepared for life, burdened from childhood with highly strained expectations, lacking the ordinary course of education, and put automatically in a class of people whose better schooling and background made him feel slighted, tried in vain to save his striving for superiority by despising rational thinking. To cling to his "style of life," he turned to irrationality, no longer controlling it by reason. When his hope of unheard-of glory had gone, he did not change his style, but devoted himself wholly to the daydreams of his childhood. To have written the present volume is in the same direction towards his goal of uniqueness, he indulged in imagination, in a grandeur that in his time, real life had denied him. [17, p. 133]

Nijinsky achieved greater recognition and fame than anyone in ballet before or since, *but that was not enough*. Therefore, he retreated into his own private world, the world of the schizophrenic, where there was no need to reason, and where there was no one else around to remind him of his failures. By rejecting reasoning, to Adler, Nijinsky embarked on a course of what he called "purposive irrationality."

What seems so illuminating about this is that ironically perhaps only in the behavior of the psychotic or of the genius, may we see the barest glimpse of the manifestations of a single unified goal, if at all. On the other hand, Adler presupposes a similar single-minded creativity and drive in all of us. Whether apparent or not, such a concept may suggest a possible explanation as to why the human personality appears to be one of the few consistent manifestations in this most inconstant world.

Chapter Three

The Paradox of Laws

FURTHER OBSERVATIONS ON THE FICTIVE GOAL

As mentioned in the previous chapter, the concept of the fictive final goal still does not appear to be understood, even by many Adlerians today, and has been almost completely ignored by other psychologists and philosophers in the field as well. It does at least offer one explanation of the principle behind the almost miraculous self-initiated organization that appears to guide us through our sometimes chaotic environment—a principle that on one hand suggests a law of nature. At the same time, this striving leads us to set a goal of what literally amounts to "perfection," which in effect would nullify all the laws as we know them if this goal were ever to be reached. But if we do it at all, perhaps we reach the goal only through the distorted imagination of the psychotic. In reality, there is a constant struggle between our perceptions of what we desire and what society and nature is willing to give us.

In this process we also try to formulate our own laws, both as individuals and as societies. Paradoxically, we then pay far more attention to our self-ordained rules than to the virtually immutable physical laws to which we are endlessly subject and which we, for the most part, take for granted. Until recently, scientists have considered many of these laws to be absolute, at least on the basis of research and evidence perceived through our normal five senses. But there are factors regarding these laws, particularly in the way in which we try to deal with them and avoid them, that seem very relevant to our studies of human personality.

The Law of Motion

Perhaps the law which influences our temporal lives the most immediately and profoundly is the law of motion. From birth until death, the necessity for survival (perhaps another law itself), ordains that the human body be in ceaseless, internal and external motion. Inhibiting that movement severely at any stage during this process (particularly when the individual is in his later years), hastens the process of decay and death. Rather surprisingly it has only been a matter of the last twenty to thirty years that medical science has begun to recognize and utilize this law as it pertains to physical fitness and recovery from severe illness. Even after death the body undergoes movement—the process we call physical decomposition and decay, when other organisms supersede those which have kept the body "alive." If there is such a thing as a spirit, independent of the body, it perhaps also moves off to another sphere, the nature of which is still unknown—though the source of virtually endless speculation by thinkers, theologians, and even some scientists. Also, all of us, whether living or dead, are subject to a series of motions that we do not feel, but which constantly affect us. These are such as the rotation of the earth around the sun, rotation of the earth around its axis, and the movement of the solar system toward or away from other galaxies, depending upon which scientific view one takes. There is also even a more obscure and little known motion, where every 26,000 years the North Pole makes a rotation in respect to its axis pointing toward certain stars. However, a possible exception may exist, even for this law. In deepest space, in the massive voids where galaxies may be billions of miles apart, there may be no motion. Yet space has characteristics of its own. From our observations and space explorations we have learned that it is utterly dark, has a constant temperature, no friction, and transmits (or perhaps does not interfere with) the movement of light, radio waves, and nuclear radiation, but not sound. It may even have its own movement, but we have not arrived at any conclusions to this effect. It may have other properties, the nature of which we are not yet aware. It may also be the only entity in the universe that has no movement of its own, so even this law may have exceptions.

The Law of Change

Another law which might also be considered as nearly absolute is the law of change, though the same may be said about this law as with the law of movement regarding deep space. Nothing is apparently ever the same from one instant to another. A piston moving up and down in a cylinder never touches the same part of the cylinder at any given stroke. The differences, if they could be measured at all, might be in inexpressibly minute fractions of a millimeter. Another way of illustrating this in human behavior might be called the "law of transactions," which reflects the relationship between individuals, particularly between those in a given family. It may appear, particularly to therapists who listen to endless repetitive discussions of what seem to be the same static activities going on in a given relationship, that nothing is changed. But there are always subtle alterations taking place in each encounter. The advent of a new family member in the group in any given family dramatically alters the structure and way in which each family member relates to one another.

The Use of Time

We have invented time as a means of measuring both motion and change. We attempt also to make time static by postulating past and future as fixed entities. But because motion is as ceaseless as change, the past is irrevocably gone. The present is inexorably moving into the future, so only the past can be truly considered static. But in our imagination, we postulate a goal in the future that is still only the conceptualized result of what has happened in the past, yet we still try to see both as fixed entities. *I saw George yesterday, and we will conclude our business deal tomorrow*. In similar ways, particularly if the experience is enjoyable, we even try to hold back the present. In a way then, we are able to do this again in our imagination. We visualize such an experience over and over, record it in books, films, or audio tapes. But in each instance, the memory is momentary; the moment itself is gone, and must be remembered over again in order to be experienced. So, motion and change are still going on interminably, despite our efforts to slow them down or halt them.

The Law of Dissimilarity

Perhaps the third law of this kind is dissimilarity. No one atom appears to be totally like another, as are no two single cells or individuals identical. Although identical twins share the same genetic heritage and often astonishing degrees of communication as well as joint habitual behavior, they are still separate in many ways. Should we ever be successful in cloning human beings, as has been theorized by genetic researchers, the clones may be closer to their original than are identical twins, but they will still be different.

Heisenberg's Uncertainty Principles

Up until the present century, most scientists tended to consider most of the laws described, particularly those such as motion, change, gravity, centrifugal force, and torque, as virtually absolute, with the relationships between them deterministic and unvariable. Up until nearly the nineteenth century, these laws—which came most from teachings of the early Greeks and were incorporated into early Christian beliefs—eventually became accepted by theologians of that day as of divine origin, and therefore immutable. Those who disputed these laws were branded as heretics, and tortured or put to death unless they renounced such beliefs. Even the Protestant reformation allowed little deviation from this dogma until the advent of the industrial technology and education in the late eighteenth century. Still, most scientists accepted the doctrines of universal causality and determinism until well into this century. In 1927, Werner Heisenberg [45], as a result of his experiments on the activity of electronic particles surrounding the atom, virtually demolished the concept of the causality which had seen few challenges for more than 2,000 years. His major thesis was that the momentum and position of these electrons could not be measured simultaneously with complete precision because observing the phenomena apparently alters their position and momentum of the electrons, at the moment of visualization.

As a result of Heisenberg's thinking, most scientists today have altered their research findings to explain them in terms of statistical probability rather than assumed fact.

The Quest for Certainty

In a recent book concerning Heisenberg's uncertainty theory, Gordon Reece outlines what he considers to be the psychological need for certainty and an essential desire to believe in causality. He says regarding the preadolescent child's view of his surroundings,

It is of little or no relevance to what extent the child's desire to impose a logical structure on the external world is in some sense innate, and to what extent it is a function of his upbringing. The only point of real significance is the *universality* of this desire, and its intensity. If it is a consequence of the direction of the child's thinking by the external world, and in particular by the adults in that world, this is a remarkable tribute to our ability to mold children in our image. There is, however, little evidence for such a view: it seems much more likely that we are born with a hefty predisposition towards a belief in causality and a desire for certainty. The most compelling evidence for this latter view is the fact that we can interpret the behavior of animals in much the same way as we interpret the behavior of human beings. We do not find any lack of "logic" in the behavior of chimpanzees, snakes, or even amoebae. We do not need a special vocabulary to describe the intelligence of animals; indeed it is standard practice to use the behavior of animals to help us understand ourselves. We *assume* that the same analysis as we know to be valid for human behavior will give correct results when applied to other creatures; we are of course imposing our own preconceptions on their behavior. Such methods have so far justified themselves by producing self-consistent results. [26, p. 365]

What is fascinating about this statement is that it is in such fundamental agreement with Adler's description of the child's attempt to overcome his "normal" feelings of inferiority more than sixty years earlier. Of course, not being a psychologist, Reece does not go nearly as far in describing how he feels the child attempts to cope with all these uncertainties he faces. As has been mentioned, Adler's concept of the fictive goal appears to be at least one concept of a self-determined formula by which the child attempts to find answers to all these baffling questions, or at least to attempt to be prepared in advance with a means of solving them.

Reece also says the following:

It is a mark of true maturity to be able to function in the absence of certainty: for example, the ability to be "good" without the certainty of ultimate retribution for one's wickedness. It is much easier to search for minor modifications than to search freely for correlations and to discover one's own truths. In practice, it is also a good deal slower and less efficient; hence the popularity of ready-made orthodoxies of every kind. [26, p. 365]

Unfortunately, the maturity which Reece suggests is needed here occurs rarely among us. Perhaps it may only be an essential characteristic of self-actualizing people, as Maslow has described them. However, the acceptance of uncertainty as a fact of life, though painful, is slowly becoming more prevalent, even though in science it is still obscured by the researcher's overuse of statistical probability as a means of somehow supporting the outmoded dogmas of causality and determinism. Though it is still statistically highly improbable that gravity and centrifugal force might at some moment cease to exist, even temporarily, and the earth will either fly out into space or into the sun, since Heisenberg's bold challenge to the dogma of centuries, the possibility may still exist. The belief that the development of the earth and life upon it has been a stable and orderly process is no longer being accepted by many scientists. The newer theories suggest that the growth, not only of the earth, but of the entire universe, has been characterized by many uncertainties and physical catastrophes, the nature of which we are only beginning to understand. Perhaps a growing degree of the inner turmoil that affects us all as human beings is this realization that *nothing* is certain, except some of our beliefs which may merely be fantasies, rather than determinable facts of existence.

The Law of Cooperation

Man, in his almost frantic quest for ultimate certainty, has also conceived of rules of behavior that he has had the temerity to consider as absolute, whether these are laws or premises, principles, or even ideals. Adler formulated what Dreikurs later called "the first social law," the "iron law of cooperation" or "co-living" as Adler termed it. The premise on which Adler's law was based is the virtually absolute interdependence of human beings upon one another for survival. The human infant would perish within a short time if not fed and clothed by someone else. During the long, painful process of development and growth to maturity— the longest and slowest of any living beings on this planet—the child must learn to cooperate, to give love, to share it with others, or he will perish emotionally if not physically. Of course, a few examples have been found where children were lost in the wilderness and apparently reared by animals. Though a number of such children have been found who survived, their physical and mental behavior seemed to be more like the animals who reared them, rather than human.

Because we are unlike other animals in this respect, we do not allow the weak to perish, so our mental hospitals and prisons are full of people who have never learned to cooperate or to love. But it would seem to be almost a law in itself that, given a clear choice as a young child, few of these individuals would have chosen to end up where they are at this time. It appears also to be true that there is just as cruel a penalty for those who are not incarcerated, but choose to evade cooperation and love, and who usually end up being rejected by most of their peers, with generally disastrous consequences. At times, two neurotics may find ways in which to relate to one another in their particular basis of cooperativeness, however negative. They may live their lives together in such a relationship, but on the other hand, there would seem to be few who could witness this objectively and wish to emulate it. There is, of course, another possible law implicit in this—that every act has its consequence—those acts that are loving and cooperative appear to be far more satisfactory to those involved than for those who behave oppositely. Ironically, this may seem to imply causality, though an absolute interpretation of this may never be able to be effectively verified.

Although it would seem obvious to most of us that such a rule, if not necessarily a law of cooperation, would be an eminently desirable one to obey, but the degree to which it is violated, almost at the same time it is being observed, again appears to show that we often try to avoid cooperation even though it is essential to our survival. Adler contended emphatically that those who refute the rules of cooperation leave little behind that other people want to remember—and that this was the measure by which violators of the law would be judged. Of course, many more of us recall Christ more vividly than Nero, but the fact that Nero is still remembered does bring some doubts about Adler's penalty as being absolute. Perhaps it is that emotionally charged events are remembered be they positive or negative. On the other hand, humanity may find out in the next hundred years or sooner whether a possible nuclear holocaust may prove the law of cooperation to be as valid as Adler and Dreikurs have proposed.

The Law of Equality

In one of his pronouncements, Dreikurs also broadened the original Adlerian formulation to conceptualize the idea of a law of equality. There appears to be little doubt that in those areas of the world where food and sustenance are not the overwhelming concern, the movement toward equality of expression appears to be growing. Unfortunately, those who rule a large part of the Earth's population appear to have become so insulated from the consequences of their behavior that many of them may live their lives without being directly aware that such a principle exists at all. The recent emergence of most of the independent nations of Africa confirms to a considerable degree that the brief moments of freedom enjoyed by inhabitants of these countries did not last long, largely because most of their leaders were incapable of governing in a democracy—or for that matter, even understanding a society that is only partially equal, such as ours. Paradoxically, and despite its enormous appeal, the concept of equality is really only an ideal because we are not entirely alike. Each of us is inferior or superior to anyone else in some capacity, but the notion of equal rights for all has enough validity to become a powerful goal for which to strive. Yet in many ways we treat equality as a law within itself, to which all of us must adhere.

The Limitations of Human Thought

There are two other principles that in some way might be called laws as well, and with which most of us must deal during the course of our lifetime. The first is that we are inextricably bound in a social relationship and must cope with it in some way in accordance to the demands of others, rather than just depending on our own whims. The second principle is that with the exception of those laws which govern our survival, most of our decisions are based on predictions of what is likely to happen tomorrow or next year. But, the way we govern ourselves in respect to those around us, particularly to those with whom we are close, will determine to a tremendous extent what tomorrow will be like if and when it comes.

Perhaps some of this can serve to explain the astonishing creativity and diversity of human thought. Being the weakest and slowest to reach maturity of all living organisms on this planet, we have developed thought to the degree that we have become aware that some of us can communicate with one another without using any of the five known senses. Some also believe we can actually move ourselves mentally and physically from future through present to past, alter or move objects by thought alone to visit other dimensions known only in our imaginations, and communicate with the dead. Though only extrasensory perception has survived scientific research of sufficient rigor to be considered a probability, proponents of these other presumed powers are just as firm in believing that their experiences are as real as those supposedly suggested by the scientific data. Of course, we can do all these things in our dreams and fantasies. The only real question is whether we are imagining that we can do all this or whether such a phenomenon is really taking place.

Paradoxically, the only entity that we may be able to conceptualize—because we still do not know what thought really is—that can, in its operations, transcend or at least temporarily nullify the laws or rules we have discussed, is human consciousness. In our fantasies and dreams we can move anywhere, suspend time and distance, create new horizons, new loves, new visions of the present and future. Yet, even here we are bound by what we have learned from the past experiences, by the limitations of our intelligence, and by the goals we have set for ourselves.

We may never know for sure, but it seems that all of us, at one time or another, would like to suspend these rules which affect us and reach the "frictionless paradise" that Lydia Sicher suggested. In our imagination we can do this, if only for the moment. If there is a purpose in evolution which follows Smuts's conception of greater holism and greater complexity at the same time, possibly Adler's goal of perfection may be seen as a description of the process of evolution leading toward such an imagined future, as well as its ultimate objective.

Chapter Four

The Style of Life

Adler's concept of the style of life is probably the most fundamental to his entire system, yet concrete or specific description of it cannot really be found in his writings. Part of the reason for this may be found in the nature of the changes that Adler made in his own philosophy in the years between his first major writings on personality before 1908, to the final evolution of his theory of social interest in the early 1920s. One of the significant changes in his beliefs was his realization that the basic human drive was not superiority over others, but significance, or feelings of worth and belonging with others. At various times, according to the Ansbachers, Adlerians have equated the style of life with the "self" or "ego," man's own personality, the unity of personality, individuality, individual form of creative activity, the method of facing problems, an opinion about one's self and the problems of life, and the whole attitude of life, as well as others. Perhaps the best generalization of the style of life might be that it is the sum total of all of the individual's attitudes, aspirations, and striving which lead him in the direction toward his goal of believing he has significance in the eyes of others. According to Adler, the individual cannot believe he is significant unto himself until he believes he is significant in the eyes of others. Perhaps his own best description of the style of life is contained in the following statement:

The child is constantly confronted with a fresh and overbearing problem which he sees can be solved neither by conditioned reflexes nor by innate ability. It would be extremely hazardous to expose a child who is equipped with only conditioned reflexes or with innate abilities to test on a world which is continuously raising new problems. The solution to the greatest problem would always be up to the never-resting creative mind. This remains pressed in the path of the child's style of life, as does everything that has a name in the various schools of psychology, such as instincts, impulses, feelings, thinking, attitudes toward pleasure and displeasure, finally love and social interest. The style of life commands all forms of expression, as the whole commands the part. [8, p. 174]

Perhaps in a way, the style of life could be likened to a great symphony wherein all the various melodies performed by diverse instruments combine into a unified and self-contained movement. Though each individual's style of life is essentially unique, according to Adler, there are certain fundamental manifestations of it which are similar for everyone.

FUNDAMENTALS OF THE STYLE OF LIFE

The Style of Life Is Holistically and Internally Self-Consistent

What this means is that according to Adler, *all* of the psychological processes going on within the individual are devoted to reaching the single, highly abstract, fictive goal. The implications of this concept, even though the term style of life as described and utilized by many psychologists today, have not been adequately understood by most disciplines. The modern Gestalt therapists today for example seem to view personality as a unity, but then insist on dealing primarily with emotions as separate from the intellect, as if there were no distinguishable relationship between the two. Of course, the implications of this concept have consequences that few individuals are totally willing to accept, which is perhaps one important reason why Adlerian philosophy is not more thoroughly understood or accepted. To Adler, emotions are the *result* not the creation of our attitudes and exist for the purpose of reinforcing a particular belief and not in inducing it. An example of this can be clearly illustrated. If an adult without prior knowledge is shown a black newspaper headline that states, "War Declared! New York, London, Moscow Destroyed by Nuclear Bombs," one could imagine the fear and horror this would provoke. But, to a three-year-old child or a New Guinea tribesman, such a message would only be some black marks on a piece of paper. The emotion aroused might be curiosity or even indifference, but not fear without an *interpretation* of what such a headline means. Of course, the role of emotions in enhancing the quality of our lives is undeniable, but their use, whether to induce pleasure or pain in, is still a purposive act. Through the bodily process, emotions promote effects in many physical ways; and just as attitudes and beliefs, emotions can also be considered cognitive processes.

Private Logic

Perhaps what also makes the concept of the style of life difficult to grasp is that often to others the behavior of an antisocial or even psychotic individual may seem bizarre, inconsistent, and entirely against his own welfare in relationship to the social environment in which he is functioning. But, according to Adler, *to the individual*, at that moment it is not. Even suicide, considered the ultimate form of self-destruction, may at a given time represent to the individual the only satisfactory method of dealing with what to him is an intolerable situation. However, to explain such attitudes and behavior which might not only be antisocial, but against the welfare of the individual, Adler formulated the term "private logic" (as distinguished from what we call communal logic or common sense), which he also at various times termed as "private sense," "private intelligence," "private world," "personal intelligence," and "isolated intelligence." According to Dreikurs, who used the term private logic extensively in his teaching and writings, Adler considered it to be the individual's answer, in a neurotic, psychotic, or unusual way, to the demands of social life and social living. Whereas the psychologically mature individual's attempts to reach his goal *coincide* to a reasonable degree with the rights and welfare of others, his internal logic can be communal logic as well. But when he does not see life in the light of objectivity and common sense, but according to his own private view of what he believes life should be, he attempts to solve his problem in a self-centered way, by attempting to dominate others and force them to do his bidding, or by avoiding what would be his normal social tasks in life. In the most extreme cases Adler suggested that the psychotic, by withdrawing to his own private world, believes that his private logic is unassailable and that he has reached his goal.

However, it must be recognized that interpreting what is true in communal logic is sometimes very difficult. Communal logic may vary in many respects from one culture to another; consequently what might be considered private logic in one culture or era may not be in another. For example, almost until the middle of the nineteenth century, the practice of slavery was considered to be an acceptable mode of community behavior. Those who disagreed with this view were often severely persecuted. Even today, in most Arab countries, women are still considered as virtual chattels and the property of their fathers or husbands. The recent brutal execution of a princess in Saudi Arabia and her lover for adultery is a shocking reminder that what is communal logic in one culture may be the opposite in others.

Obviously, the term used by Adler and Dreikurs must be interpreted in this light. A very mature individual may oppose the practices of a whole culture and his behavior may seem illogical at a given time, but his view of the welfare of all may well be more accurate, even though he is often severely persecuted for his views. At that moment, what might be termed his "human logic" leads him to such a view, even though he may be risking his welfare or even his life for his beliefs. The stories of a number of such brave and enlightened persons has been aptly delineated in John Kennedy's book, *Profiles in Courage*. Sadly, all too often at the time, the true maturity of the views of such individuals may be termed private logic even by scholars and psychologists who are limited and do not see the prejudice in their own beliefs.

The Individual Acts in Accordance with What He Perceives or Believes Reality to Be, Not What It Actually Is or Perhaps What Others Perceive It to Be

This concept is widely accepted today, as what the Gestaltists call a "behavioral environment" or the "phenomological field." As was mentioned previously, Adler leaned heavily on Hans Vaihinger's philosophy of "as if" to support his concept, which at the time he called "tendentious apperception." There is, of course, intense controversy in philosophy today as to whether such a thing as "reality" exists in and by itself, or is simply a matter of what we perceive. However, as we spend most of our time behaving according to our perceptions, there seems little chance that this controversy will be resolved to the satisfaction of either side.

The Logic of Behavior

The difficulty in dealing with private logic is, of course, the process by which a neurotic or psychotic tends to reach his goal. According to Adler, as long as a person treats his interpretation of what he sees as real, he will act accordingly. Consequently, we can only deal with his behavior and try to imagine what mistaken perceptions have led to it, if it is considered unacceptable or antisocial.

Of course, with respect to perceptions of our environment around us, those who are relatively normal individuals agree with most others in a similar culture with respect to the objective surroundings that one can see, hear, or touch. But this desk I am looking at might be viewed as a piece of green cheese by a psychotic who may try to eat it, or as a cave in which to hide by a small child, or a source of firewood by a primitive tribesman. What is interesting, these perceptions may not be unreal or illogical when viewed as simply a means of fitting the object into the framework of one's own perception.

But in personal and social relationships where there is so little that can be truly considered objective is where we have the most difficulty in perceiving accurately, or at least in conformance with what we *believe* is "logic." There seems to be a fairly universal characteristic that humans tend to underrate their own significance in the eyes of others. With few notable exceptions, our friends and associates think better of us than we do, and in a close relationship such as marriage, each partner has a certain degree of bias, often erroneous, to what his or her opposite partner thinks of him or her and expects from him or her. The opposite partner brings another set of biases to bear on the situation. The closeness and satisfaction of the relationship usually depends on how well these two sets of perceptions can be accommodated to one another. With such a set of imponderables, it is a wonder that any close relationship lasts at all. It is true that in societies that are becoming more equal, the breakup of such relationships, unfortunately, appears to be increasing. But relationships exist and always will because we all share an overwhelming need to belong and to be loved; accordingly, most of us are willing to subordinate or at least put up with some of the disagreeable attitudes we feel our partners possess in order to try and reach such closeness.

The Style of Life Is Not Only Internally Self-Consistent, but Also Longitudinally Constant

Generally speaking, according to Adler, once someone's goal concept has been formulated, which occurs sometime between the ages of six and eight, that person may change occupations, physical environments, or partners, but the essentials of the style of life remain constant. Adler's concept of the prototype, based on the child's early observation and interpretation of behavior of those individuals around him, gives us some clues as how to understand this. The child's choice of occupations, as has been mentioned earlier, often fits this prototype—though it may not be based on any one individual that the child has met, or for that matter might be like anyone he has known. Adler makes an interesting reference to this with respect to his own life:

When I was five, I became ill with pneumonia and was given up by the physician. A second physician advised treatment just the same, and in a few days I became well again. In the joy over my recovery, there was talk for a long time about the mortal danger in which I was supposed to have been. From that time on, I recall always thinking of myself in the future as a physician. This means that I had set a goal from which I could expect an end to my childhood distress, my fear of death. Clearly, I expected more from the occupation of my choice than I would accomplish. The overcoming of death and the fear of death is something I should not have expected from human, but only Divine accomplishment. Reality, however, demanded action so I was forced to modify my goal by changing the conscious form of my guiding fiction to satisfy reality. So, I came to choose the occupation of physician to overcome death and the fear of death.

The following experience dates from the time of my choosing my occupation, about my fifth year. The father of a playmate asked me what I wanted to become and I answered, "a doctor." To this, the man who possibly had unfortunate experiences with a physician, answered, "in that case, one should hang you right away from the nearest lamppost." On account of my regulative guiding, this comment left me cold. I believe that I thought at the time I would become a good physician, toward whom no one should have hostile feelings. Soon after, it struck me that this man, a lamp maker, had his trade rather than me uppermost in his mind. After that, the determination to become a doctor never left me. I could never picture myself taking up any other profession, even the fascinating lure of art, despite the fact that I had considerable abilities in various forms of music. But music was not enough to turn me from my chosen path. [18, p. 199–200]

What is most interesting about this statement is that although two of the three experiences that Adler describes in his dealing with physicians were decidedly negative, he chose the occupation of physician, a healing person who defeats death at least temporarily if not permanently. With respect to the constancy of behavior, Adler further stated,

When a prototype, that early personality which embodies the goal, is formed in the line of direction to establish, an individual becomes definitely oriented. It is this fact which enables us to predict what will happen in later life. The individual's perceptions are, from then on, bound to fall into a groove established by the line of direction. A child will not perceive given situations in exact existence, but under the prejudice of his own interests. From now on the world is seen through a stable scheme of perceptions, experiences are interpreted before they are accepted and the interpretation always accords with the original meaning of life. But if this meaning is gravely mistaken, even if the approach to our problems and tasks brings continuous misfortune and agony, it is never easily relinquished. [18, p. 189]

RESEARCH ON CONSTANCY OF PERSONALITY

Though many theses have been advanced, both pro and con, regarding the stability of personality, the research on this concept has been sparse and somewhat conflicting. The most significant early post–World War II sources, David Kretch and R. S. Krutchfield [48], both strongly supported Adler's contention that even under conditions of severe mental and emotional deprivation, the basic personality attributes of the individual did not tend to change materially.

If this is true, then what about the goals of psychotherapy? Which essentially attempt to create such changes in personality that are necessary to help the individual to live a more satisfied life? This is still an area where no firm consensus has been achieved in our psychological thinking. There are still many who consider change to be a day-to-day process, though few will deny that accomplishing a change in personality with severely disturbed or psychotic individuals is an enormously difficult, if not impossible task. The experiments with electroshock therapy, certain types of drugs, or even surgical procedures such as lobotomy, appear to have had success in only a limited number of patients. Adler's statement about the possibility of curing Nijinsky would not seem to reinforce this belief in the essential stability of the style of life, even under enormous emotional threat. It is unfortunate that more research has not been made among less-disturbed individuals to throw more light on this controversial issue.

Chapter Five

Holism and the Unconscious Mind

THE CONSCIOUS AND UNCONSCIOUS MINDS

Perhaps one of the most puzzling of phenomena to students of personality theory today is the relationship between the so-called conscious and unconscious minds. Subconscious and preconscious levels have been added to this dialogue so that all of the operations of the mind outside of direct consciousness are placed in one grab bag labeled "unconscious." This includes the entire range of the functions of the body that are controlled by the mind, along with our direct awareness and also some aspects of personality which are much less easily defined. What further complicates the matter is the psychoanalytic theory of Freud, who has alleged that the unconscious mind is likened to a vast reservoir, which he called the "id," and from which emerged what he called "libidinal impulses," the main purpose of which was to achieve self-gratification, whether at the expense of someone else's welfare or not. Freud then theorized two other entities in the personality, the "ego" and the "superego," both of which are conscious and unconscious at various times. In his view, the mind is a battleground between the id, represented by the libidinal impulses, and the superego, represented by the individual's responses to the demands of society. According to Freud, most of these impulses are not in our control. The ego is seen to predominantly exist as a mediator between these two forces.

Freud also suggested that the individual represses desires which are unacceptable to the superego and eliminates them from conscious awareness, but he did see that they still continue to play a part in the individual's behavior. They often create anxieties, the nature of which the person was not consciously aware, such as slips of the tongue, compulsions, obsessions, and consciously unacceptable "accidents" of thought that somehow "happen" without the person being able to control them. He also formulated a system of what he called unconscious defense mechanisms, such as projection, obsessive–compulsive behavior, some types of phobias, and psychosomatic symptoms, which, though often annoying or even frightening to the individual, are more socially accepted than (at least in his opinion) his instinctual sexual or destructive desires. Though Freud's theory of repression is still widely regarded as his most monumental discovery, his concepts of the id, ego, and superego have lost much of their acceptance today.

Adler's View

Early in his relationship with Freud, Adler disagreed completely with Freud's concept of the duality of man's nature. It was probably this concept, plus his insistence that sex was not at the basis of all neurotic phenomena that led to Adler's leaving the Freudian society in 1911. By 1914, Adler had completely accepted what he called "views" that attempt to grasp living phenomena and the variations within as connected wholes—physically, philosophically, and psychologically. Basically, this suggests that the whole is greater than the sum of its parts. Adler called his concept "comparative individual psychology," which starts with the assumption of the unity of the individual and then attempts to attain a picture of this unified personality as a variant of the manifestations of life and forms of expression. Individual traits are then compared with one another, brought to a common plane, and finally fused together to form a composite portrait that is individualized.

In 1912, Wertheimer [75] demonstrated another aspect of the holistic concept in his experiments with visual perception. His theory utilized the motion picture as an example. Actually, the motion picture as we see it is a series of still photographs moving in sequence with an opaque frame inserting itself between the movement of one still to another. Visually, the eye and brain ignores the blackened out phase and sees the stills as movement. Out of this came Wertheimer's statement that "there are wholes in behavior which are not determined by individual elements, but by where the part processes themselves are determined by the intrinsic nature of the whole."

Some years later the movement which Wertheimer started, and was followed by other leading psychologists such as Koffka, Kohler, and Kurt Lewin, has become an approach which has been variously termed organismic psychobiological configuration, utilizing Gestalt or holistic principles. This was a movement to which Adler belonged, though there was little cross-reference between him and the earlier Gestaltists. Adler had concluded that all the resources of the body, including both the conscious and unconscious minds, were devoted toward the single purpose of attempting to reach the fictive holistic goal which the individual had established in childhood. Adler also acknowledged that William Stern had also arrived at a similar conclusion some years earlier in respect to the holistic nature of personality.

HOLISM AND EVOLUTION

Some years later, Adler also called attention to another theory of holism which he felt greatly reinforced his own concepts concerning the unity of the personality, but which had much broader implications as well. This was described in a book written by Jan Christian Smuts, one-time premier of South Africa, in 1922. In his book, Smuts proposed that all of the universe, from the tiniest atom to the vast galaxies, were governed by two fundamental laws: holism and diversity. Thus, as the atom revolving around with its companions forms a compound, planets revolving around the sun and the galaxies moving in relation to each other all demonstrate this process. He also suggested there was a continuum between organic and inorganic life as we know it. In such a system, the human being is not whole unto himself, but in cooperation with other groups, and forms such groups, the sum total characteristics of which are more than the contributions of a single individual. Evolution was seen as a constant process leading towards greater complexity but, at the same time, greater holism throughout the cosmos [66].

There is little question that the holistic concept has been greatly strengthened by the experiments of Wertheimer, Koffka, Kohler, Kurt Lewin, and others, as well as by those who researched and developed the theory of homeostasis, discussed in an earlier chapter.

Though Adler accepted the idea that there were ideas that existed outside of the consciousness, to him it was more a matter of the levels of awareness over which he felt the conscious mind was the ultimate ruler. But it is important to understand how, in his view, the process works, to know how we arrive at certain concepts, and why behavior is as consistent as it is in the face of valid arguments to the contrary.

LEVELS OF AWARENESS

In his earliest discoveries, Adler suggested that all our physical and psychological resources function cooperatively in a holistic fashion to insure the survival of the individual. The functioning of the mind operated on so-called "levels," extending all the way from self-consciousness and so called preconscious awareness to such functions as digestion and circulation of the blood, the functions of which most of the time we have little or no conscious awareness of at all. In general, it was felt we had little conscious control over these functions as well, except that we could always stop them by committing suicide. However, by utilizing a relatively new technique called biofeedback, we have learned that individuals can exercise a considerable degree of control over blood pressure, the rate of heartbeat, and numerous other bodily functions with specifically conscious goals. In one characteristic experiment, subjects are hooked up to a machine that used a series of light flashes followed by a pinup picture whenever the blood pressure dropped by itself. During these experiments, it was found that when decreased blood pressure occurred it was followed by visualizations of the flashing lights and pinup pictures without the use of the machine. Hospitals have also used a similar technique in restoring these functions. In treating a patient who was paralyzed in one arm, a certain pattern was flashed on the screen each time he moved his good arm. Eventually, by repeating this visual picture over and over again, the patient eventually learned to transfer this process to the paralyzed arm. At least 75 percent of the patients thus treated recovered partial to full control of the paralyzed limb.

The "Automatic" Processes

Though at the time Adler was concerned primarily of consciousness in regard to personality, he saw that though the conscious mind was the ultimate ruler, there were so-called "unconscious" processes that were responses to certain types of stimuli, to which individuals had trained themselves to respond without being consciously aware of the reasons behind the response. This can be explained best by describing the learning of motion skills such as playing the piano or driving a car. When one is first confronted with a piano and a sheet of notes, the learner first has to consciously think of the note on the page and then transfer with his finger to a corresponding note on the piano. Each subsequent note must be dealt with singularly, and at the beginning the process is painfully slow and cumbersome. But after a certain period of practice, merely looking at the note is sufficient to be able to find the corresponding key without conscious effort, and eventually just thinking of the notes in the melody produce an automatic response of the keys being pressed. The memory of this process had been transferred to the unconscious mind. Another example is when driving a car, the person can be thinking of something entirely different other than control of the car, but still remain safely on the road.

Peripheral versus Central Thinking

There is another mental process that works somewhat like the function of the eye. If we fix out central vision on an object and spread our arms out to our sides, we can still see our hands almost parallel, though somewhat less clearly. This is called peripheral vision and is vitally necessary to driving a car as well as many other trained motor functions. Adler realized that the same process—now called "preconscious" rather than "unconscious" perception—goes on in the mind with respect to ideas and attitudes. Snygg and Combs [68] some years later discovered this phenomenon and labeled it "subliminal perception." By use of a machine called a tachistoscope, they measured how quickly subjects could identify a word or picture flashed on a screen at speeds too rapid to see and record consciously at first. The rates of flash were then slowed down until the subjects could consciously identify a word or picture. However, they also found that certain unacceptable or "taboo" words or pictures were recalled by many subjects later than neutral or pleasant ones. Also, by using a machine similar to a polygraph, with some subjects it was discovered that when certain unacceptable words were shown, the machine demonstrated a galvanic skin response before the subject was able to consciously identify the word or picture. For a while this discovery spawned a host of fanciful notions about its possible use. At theaters, patrons were shown pictures of popcorn and candy, all flashed at subliminal speeds on the screen before and after the movie. It was discovered that sales did not appreciably increase as a result of these attempts at mental manipulation, and that part of the movement soon died out.

The Psychological Nature of Awareness

This aspect of perception, when translated to psychological terms, takes on enormous importance. The child who is a victim of a brutal father or uncaring mother can train himself to respond to this treatment in ways that are as efficient as he can imagine. Perhaps in the case of the father, simply avoiding him as much as possible minimizes the risk of being physically hurt. This process can be trained to the point where it becomes automatic, therefore outside of awareness. Such a vigilant function, as the child grows to adulthood, also may be subject to generalizations, because being outside of consciousness, it is not subject to change without conscious reinterpretation. Any man who resembles the child's father will be someone to avoid. If the child is a girl, the grownup woman as an adult may consciously see other men as being not like her father, but the lack of awareness of how she has trained herself will present a more powerful influence, so that it will become a habit pattern that will constantly provide her with warning signals against achieving too close a relationship to any adult male. Often, if the subject maintains contact with men at all, she may only be comfortable with those who are in some ways unacceptable as possible permanent partners. At the same time, she nearly always manages to find fault with a potentially acceptable man or devises ways to make herself unacceptable to those who really do count. In such situations, the subject develops a defense mechanism against becoming aware of the real reasons for her rejecting certain men. If she does seek therapy with an Adlerian, inquiring into the relationship she experienced with her parents and other children in the family affords an important diagnostic clue as to why this behavior is being maintained. Nearly always an important part of changing such a trained attitude would be the attempt of the therapist to show her that not all men will treat her as did her father. She must learn to consciously become aware of certain habitual behaviors which stem from her initial feelings of rejection. Some of the more specific ways of dealing with this will be discussed later in this book.

Resistance to Change

Part of the difficulty here lies in the fact that the longer time we spend training ourselves for the unconscious level to react in a certain way to certain influences, with which we come in contact, the more difficult it becomes to change at someone else insistence. As a consequence, we invoke all sorts of defense mechanisms to keep us from really looking at the mistaken aspects of our attitude. Much skill from the therapist is needed in helping to penetrate these mechanisms in order to help the patient see the real issue.

In any event, viewing this hypothetical case as a manifestation of holistic principles, however abhorrent the girl's behavior might seem, and even if it could lead to suicide or psychosis, to Adler, her behavior was viewed as *purposive and logical*. Dreikurs, if considering her case, would have termed such attempts to protect herself from the hurt she felt was inflicted upon her as a child, as her "private logic," which is more in accord with her reality and is based on the mistaken goal. The mistaken *premise* assumes that if she attempts to fall in love with or become intimate with any man, that he will ultimately reject or hurt her, as did her father. Even the inner turmoil of conflict that such an attitude might engender is viewed as a *purposive* attempt to avoid becoming aware of the consequences of a mistaken lifestyle.

METHODS OF CURE

It is interesting to note that although Freud's conceptions of a relationship between the conscious and unconscious mind is diametrically opposed to those of Adler, his later attempts at cures were in some ways similar. Freud's first attempts to gain his client's awareness of the problem behind the symptom was accomplished through hypnosis, where he regressed the individual back to the stage in childhood where the trauma that Freud believed had brought on the symptoms was to have taken place. In some cases he was successful in eliminating the particular symptom, only to have the patient exhibit a different one not long afterward. His next technique was to resolve the problem with the "free association" method, by which the patient was asked to lie on the couch and talk about whatever came to mind. To Freud, such a process would ultimately lead back to the original trauma that occurred in early childhood and brought about the conflict and subsequent neurosis. This technique was in some ways more successful than hypnosis, though modern psychoanalysts move much closer in Adler's direction in attempting to point out early the mistakes and perceptions that led to difficulties in relationships at the present time.

Much of the modern encounter group types of therapy, which appear to have somewhat faded out in recent years, particularly those which were started by Carl Rogers and Fritz Perls, owe much of their allegiance to Freud's early idea of catharsis through free association. In general, the motives of these groups is to help the individual "get in touch with his feelings," and to learn to express them freely, and to be able to react with other group members. Many nonverbal as well as verbal techniques have been developed to aid in this process. Adlerians in general suggest that though sometimes such groups may be very helpful for the individual who has difficulty in expressing his feelings, they are not very efficient with the more severe types of mistaken attitudes. It was Adler's belief that because attitudes are purposive, so are emotions. When the emotion is used to reinforce an attitude, whatever it might be—joyful or tragic—releases of negative feelings such as anger or fear, in a group setting, may not result in a change of a mistaken attitude unless the attitude itself is thoroughly explored and revealed to the person. Also, sometimes an attitude cannot be reached except through interpretation by some other member of the group, or in discussion of the events which led up to the feelings that are expressed. In many encounter groups, such types of behavior are forbidden.

Consequently, the release of the feelings may be temporarily cathartic but may not be much help in removing the source of the negative feelings and mistaken goals.

In general, however, it has become apparent that the modern trend of many of the disciplines that are popular today, such as transactional analysis, existentialism, and the teachings of William Glasser [40] and Albert Ellis [37], is to move dramatically away from Freud's dualism toward the holistic phenomenological concepts expressed by Adler.

Chapter Six

Equality and Masculine Protest

Equality—there is perhaps no other idealized misquoted, misunderstood, and un-adhered-to principle in all human relations. Webster defines the word as the "state of being equal—exact agreement, uniformity." He also categorizes persons being equal as a "person of the same rank or condition." Of course, a contradiction immediately appears. Everyone wants to be equal with everyone else, but no one wants to be the same as anyone else. Or is it possible for anyone to be completely equal with one another in any one characteristic? Then why does the term have such a magic connotation? Equality is a fundamental principle that all democratic societies proclaim to be the right of all their constituents, yet there is no human society or community on earth, including our own, where every member of the society is treated as equally as every other member.

DOES EQUALITY EXIST AT ALL?

Many thinkers point out that as long as we are not truly intellectually, physically, or economically equal, that the concept is too vague and idealistic to ever be achieved. In one sense they are right. The infant and his limited capabilities is not equal to the average ten-year-old child, who is not equal in capacity to the adult. But if we were able to narrow the term down to what might be called "equal human *rights*," we are then on much firmer ground. However, even here in the most advanced societies, we are still far from approaching the full achievement of equal rights for all.

The early Greeks, who are credited with laying down a foundation for democratic societies to come, talked of equality among *free men*. Though this was a monumental step in the direction of human rights, it excluded women, slaves, and children from this society and left universal equality far from being realized.

JESUS CHRIST AND PERSONAL EQUALITY

Perhaps one of the earliest and most revered prophets after the Greeks, who suggested that all humans should be treated equally, was Christ. He may have been crucified more because of the universal fear of the possible consequences of his teaching than for his religious beliefs. Though the principles he espoused live today, probably more because of his preachings about human rights rather than religious dogma, the terrible irony about the movement he founded is that in later times many of the most hideous persecutions and useless wars in history have been perpetrated in the name of Christianity.

KARL MARX

It is certainly a quantum leap from the teachings of Christ to those of Marx— and there are many who will call it outright heresy to even consider both men in the same context. Yet, since Christ, no other single thinker has so dramatically influenced and changed the course of world history. And, despite his rejection of religion as a means of improving the lot of humanity, Marx *did* believe in equality in much the same way as did Christ.

The Classless Society

Though Marx conceived his philosophy and wrote his work, *Das Kapital,* in the middle of the nineteenth century, it was not until the Communist Revolution of 1917 in Russia that a society emerged based essentially on his teachings. As can be seen, the results of this revolution were far different and obviously nowhere near the equality Marx had envisioned. But Marx at least added an element which Christ had not really dealt with. His proposals attempted to demonstrate why there was so little equality or freedom on Earth, and how such an ideal "classless society" might be evolved. In his view, the exploitation of the working masses by their economic masters was at the core of the inequality and prejudices that existed. His formula for a cure was relatively simple. Simply do away with the bosses, and hand the democratic means of sustenance to the workers. When everyone became adequately clothed, fed, and housed as humans, there would be no further need for exploitation. The State would simply wither away and an ideal, classless, democratic society would emerge.

In retrospect, it seems astonishing that his ideas would have so profoundly affected the world, particularly since socialism as an economic concept was not new, and utopias even more revolutionary and simplistic than Marx's had been proposed and failed many times before. But there were two profound changes that occurred in the world that made Marx's ideas seem sensible—ideas that would have been dismissed as utter lunacy a few hundred years prior.

The first was the beginnings of societies where open dissent was not quickly suppressed, but at least tolerated. The American and French Revolutions, as well as the growth of democracy in England, generated a climate where the ways of governing were becoming open to criticism. The ideas of Rousseau and Voltaire, which were fiercely repudiated in their day, began to be sought after. The bold new movements in democracy headed by Jefferson, Washington, and Abraham Lincoln inspired a whole generation of philosophers and thinkers who felt change was needed.

The second major transformation was the Industrial Revolution, which provided a degree of technology unknown before. For the first time, man realized he could create the machines that would end his years of drudgery and endless toil with so little result.

The brilliance in Marx's concept is that he saw technology as a means to rid the world of famine, although his error may have been in believing the only means to accomplish this was through overtaking the capitalist bosses. If it could be properly controlled, his "classless society" could be achieved. In keeping with his beliefs, he also rejected religion as being a tool of the capitalistic rulers—which unfortunately in all too many instances was true—and in turn he conceived what he called "dialectical materialism" as its substitute, which virtually became in itself a religion among the millions of his followers all over the world.

A Success Story

Perhaps there is one society today where the Marxist dream might still have some chance of being fulfilled—China. Before Communism, the vast numbers of illiterate peasants in China were ruled by what amounted to little more than an enclave of dictatorial warlords and corrupt capitalists. In a country of over a billion people with relatively meager natural resources, there is virtually no starvation in China today. Of course, neither is there freedom nor democratic participation in government as we know it. Since democracy as we have enjoyed it never existed in China to begin with, it is hard to say truthfully that Communism has not bettered the lot of China's people in the last forty years comparatively. Even so, during what was termed Mao's "great leap forward," when his overly eager young Red Guards attempted to wipe out what vestiges of religion and private enterprise which remained, they failed. The stubborn peasants simply refused to turn over their meager, privately grown stocks of food to the all-embracing communes that Mao tried to institute. Many of the capitalists who ruled in the days of the Communist takeover of China still live and exist in relative affluence compared to the rest of the population. Though they do not own the factories they run, Mao was wise enough, or perhaps foolish enough as history may yet show, to see that their skills were necessary to industrialize his vast country. One example of such an individual, reported in a newspaper account, is a factory manager who rides to work in his own chauffeured limousine, lives in a luxurious apartment, and has a summer villa and assets far in excess of the average worker's. At the same time, although Chinese women and children may have more social equality than before, only a tiny minority of these committees and individual political leaders—who are themselves chosen by the hierarchy from above—have really anything to say about what goes on politically in China, or for that matter, in any other Communist country today. As we have seen, the efforts by Chinese pro-democracy students to accomplish the kind of undertaking that has happened in Russia were brutally and forcefully put down by Chinese leaders. At the same time, the Communist leaders in China have embarked on what amounts to a liberal influx of capitalism in an effort perhaps to stifle some of the restlessness of the population, and perhaps more important to increase production and income to feed and clothe their immense population. There are no real human rights in China today, but there is economic expansion on an unparalleled scale. Whether this will lead to more unrest or an accommodation that will allow the Chinese to maintain their dictatorial power is difficult to predict.

After the collapse of Communism in Russia, Russians today have more freedom than they have ever had before, but a huge number of them are economically worse off than they were under its old system. Whether a stabler, free society will eventually supplant the chaos that exists is also very difficult to predict.

As well, there exists in the world today as many other diverse brands of Communism as there are Christian religions and sects. One can almost see an analogy in how far both movements have departed from the teachings of the original prophets. There seems to be just as much difference between the rigid doctrines of the Unitarian and Methodist, or of the Catholic and Protestant right-wing churches as between Pol Pot and the late Marshall Tito. So, why cannot one say with certainty that Marx still has the answer? One possibility may be that in no society where the Communists achieved full power were they ever freely chosen by the people who inhabit it. And they were quickly thrown out of power when the opportunity arose. A minor exception was the Allende regime in Chili, but it was overthrown by a CIA-inspired coup long before the Communists were able to establish firm control of the country. Unfortunately, with few exceptions the example of how Marx's followers have behaved in these lands they now control and the degree of repression and brutality they have engendered in order to maintain their control verify conclusively that little true equality has been achieved. The State, rather than withering away as Marx suggested, has become as fully totalitarian as the most repressive right-wing dictatorships.

Where Was Marx's Error?

Whether Marx truly understood the nature of man's mistaken goals for power, his followers obviously did not, or ignored what he said. Power is only one form of control. Eliminating economic inequality unfortunately does not destroy the desire for supremacy over others.

THE HOW AND WHY OF POWER

Thus, we can see analogies in the vision of both Christ and Marx, and as well the failures of each of their beliefs in creating the world they both desired. Though this may be the most presumptuous statement in this book, perhaps one ingredient most needed to answer why both Christ and Marx failed to achieve their great ideals has been provided by Alfred Adler. Essentially, Adler was the first to truly understand why it is so difficult to accept one another as equals. Adler also has offered what in his belief was a workable means of helping people to give up the desires of power over others.

CAN WE EVER ACHIEVE TRUE EQUALITY?

Christ believed that equality could only come by faith. However, he was unable, as have been most religious leaders both past and present, to explain *why* some people believe and others just as sincere do not. Marx saw it as being achieved by force. Adler felt that true equality could only be achieved by understanding one's mistaken social perceptions and correcting them. One must learn to accept his friend, his neighbor, his wife, or his child as an equal. Most of us grow up without understanding how to treat anyone else as equal. Of course, in order to achieve this, one must understand that there are two sets of standards by which we measure equality. One is capacity, of which it can be said that we are all unequal in one way or another. The other, which is far more important, is that as humans, we all have or should have certain fundamental equal rights. This can be best exemplified in the Universal Declaration of Human Rights, which was perhaps Eleanor Roosevelt's greatest achievement in defining what are the fundamental rules that make us all truly equal. Unfortunately, it is one of the seldom remembered or utilized principles in the Charter of the United Nations. Essentially, it means that all of us should have the right to adequate unpolluted air, water, food, and a comfortable shelter, the love and respect of our fellows, and perhaps as fundamental as all of them, we should also have the right to participate openly in the decisions which govern us. In Maslow's remarkable study on self-actualization, as mentioned in the next chapter, he showed us early on that those with the highest degree of self-actualization generally spent most of their life's work trying to help others achieve the human rights to which we are all entitled. Even in the most advanced and relatively homogeneous, democratic societies, such as Sweden and Switzerland, in varying degrees there are still great disparities in equality between the various segments of society, such as those in the cases of the minority versus the majority, workers versus management, women versus men, and children versus adults. Although we could say the Swiss and Swedes are perhaps politically and economically somewhat more advanced than we, in many ways our relationships between men and women, children and adults, although far from perfect, are more advanced than theirs. However, the most significant revolution taking place in this country at present is that between men and women. Somehow, more than seventy years ago Adler anticipated this revolution, and pointed out the major reason why the sexes here are so far from equality with one another—in his concept of a masculine protest.

THE DOMINANCE OF THE MALE

With the exception of a very few societies in history—such as early Sparta and a few others that did not last very long—most of the world even today is essentially male dominated. This began in the days of the cave men. The man, being physically stronger, had to leave the cave to find the means of sustenance while the woman remained, bearing and raising the children and serving the physically superior male. Through technology and understanding of the human mind, we are now aware that men are not intellectually superior to women and in our present society it is the intellect which ultimately rules. However, men continue to try and hold on to their domination—first by physical means, then by political means, and now by a careful set of special rules, many unwritten, that are designed to keep men in the ascendent position and women as inferior. Though the advent of universal suffrage signaled the beginning of the end of domination, this elaborate set of unwritten rules still exists today. Through them, men continue to exercise control over society with methods and ways that are much more subtle than in the past. These rules affirm what Adler called the "myth of male superiority," that men were not only physically stronger, but are more logical, more rational, less emotional, more intellectual—and therefore, better than women. Women, on the other hand, were considered emotional, tender, weak, compulsive, unpredictable, all of which qualities one considered inferior even in today's democratic societies.

WHAT IS MASCULINE PROTEST?

Though the terms listed above are not necessarily the exclusive possession of or can be truthfully said to derogate either sex, the masculine ideal is still considered more desirable by both men and women. This has lead to *both* sexes striving to achieve the mythical standard of value which is still considered masculine. Today, children are reared according to this standard—boys are taught to be rough and tough, physically stronger than girls, which they still are. But they are also supposed to be more aggressive, care less about school, and get into more trouble, and are given more freedom to do so than girls. Girls are reared to be neat, clean, do well in school, help out around the house, take care of the men, and grow up to be proper young ladies. By late adolescence some change occurs. Men are trained to continue to be intellectually aggressive, but not necessarily physically so. They are supposed to become educated and become leaders of business and society. Women are allowed to have an education, but are expected to go back home, raise children, and not use the education they have achieved. Of course, though more and more women are resisting this tendency, the standard of value is still in the marketplace. Child-rearing is just as difficult and requires as much skill as any other endeavor, but our society accords it very little value. For a woman to feel worthwhile, she must compete with men in the marketplace, and be paid for doing so. Only then will she have achieved an assumed equality. We are confronted with a paradox that all of us wish to be equal, but most of us fantasize being more "equal" than anyone else, which actually means being superior to others.

Perhaps the curious phenomenon which illustrates how subtle and yet how strong this myth of masculine superiority is today is in the field of sexual relationships. Until recently, in all sexual matters, the male was in the superior position. The male was expected—in fact still is—to make the overtures, the female is supposed to be reluctant, but to "go along" in a sense. The man "had his way" with a woman. She "surrendered." Somewhere along the 1950s and later, when it was decided that sex was not solely for procreation, nor solely for the pleasure of man, men were saddled with an extra responsibility—that of making sure the woman was as satisfied as was he. The sex manuals of those days were replete with suggestions of how to conduct an elaborate sexual foreplay to arouse the woman and to control his sexual performance so that she could achieve orgasm. The woman was expected to be passive and resistant at the start but to conform, and if the man acted properly, to achieve orgasm almost as if to reward him for his successful performance.

The New Sexual Revolution

With the advent of Masters and Johnson [55] on the scene in the 1950s as the first recognized sex therapists, this concept was dealt a rather crushing blow. But in doing so, Masters and Johnson inadvertently added a new set of imperatives, quite different from the old, but still holding on to some of the elements of the status quo. Their belief was that it was not performance but anxiety which was the major problem with feeling satisfactory within a sexual relationship. The goal of sex being pleasure, it was necessary to remove this anxiety in order for successful sexual functioning to take place. Their procedures consisted primarily of a series of exercises whereby partners stimulated each other until each was able to achieve the maximum amount of pleasure. If this was not possible, the therapist secured surrogates who acted as a substitute for the partner in order to achieve the same purpose. This proved to be highly successful with some couples. However, later many therapists felt there was still something missing, and that it was the expectancy of having to perform in a certain way which really dated back to the old element of the male being aggressive and the woman being passive. There still seemed a great deal of difficulty among some people who were having sexual problems in their marriage or in their relationship.

Deviations from Masters and Johnson

At least one of the later researchers, the Berkeley Group, suggested that it was the person's resistance against having to perform when being approached by the partner which was the real issue. When they were able to verbalize their feelings, and their resistances and fears about being unable to perform adequately, very often the fears and resistances vanished.

Obviously, none of these methods could be considered as anything other than dealing with symptoms. Most sex therapists today realize that their techniques were not successful with individuals having severe neurotic or emotional difficulties between themselves. One can see in these theories, however, a notable step in the direction of sexual equality, if not equality in other matters, although their solutions to sexual problems seem overly simplistic. Authors of this particular method are quick to point out that where the more severe problems are present, individual therapy and/ or marriage counseling is necessary before the sexual inhibitions can be cured. It is true that the old male-imposed rules of behavior that guided society for so many thousand of years are no longer valid. A new set of rules must be formulated to take their place. A whole host of new techniques, ideas, faiths, fads, and fancies have sprung up to help us solve these problems. Some may see in these chapters an attempt to provide a panacea for all ailments of the human personality. Obviously, this is impossible. No one method, technique, or ideal will work with everyone. Even today there are individuals who live saintly lives, helping others, based almost strictly on principles laid down by Christ. There are people who may be doing the same thing as atheists as in following Karl Marx, but they are less evident. Perhaps, in this writer's opinion, what Adler has accomplished is to have moved us a few steps further along the road to better understanding of the internal and societal factors which have led to such difficulties in human relationships. He has also presented us with at least a systematic and pragmatic method of understanding these ills, and though somewhat less effective overall, it is still certainly a viable method of trying to solve them.

Yet, there are also forces working in opposite direction. As I mentioned before, it was Dreikurs who pointed out that the underlying motive of all human beings beyond mere survival itself was equality, and the need for it. At the time of my first encounter with him, more than thirty years ago, it was his belief that this demand was so strong that it would in democratic countries sweep away the forces of prejudice and power and create a new society where all segments have a modicum of equality, and work toward the idea of true freedom and participation for all. But in 1972, in an address before the first Individual Psychotherapy Conference sponsored by the Chicago Medical School, he pointed out that in the 1960s, many of the old traditional authoritarian values had been swept away, that the new society was indeed more free, and that young people could do practically anything their physical resources would allow them to do. However, doing away with authoritarian restraints, which up until this time had prevented people from achieving their goals, did not result in more tolerance for each other. Rather than accepting the responsibility that goes with freedom, this new generation had embarked upon a course of satisfying their wants regardless of the consequences. In his terms, he felt that we were evolving from a neurotic to a psychotic society. By illustrating this he said the psychotic is characterized by his denial of social demands and social values. In his delusions and hallucinations, he creates a world free from the demands of reality.

We find that to our great distress, that psychotic behavior is not only limited to people who are psychotic. It is a general trend of people, particularly the young, that they feel they have the right to give in to all impulses. They can do whatever they want, and if society does not let them do what they want, then society is evil and they are against it. The interesting part is that this denial of social values is done by those known to defy society. We find

among idealists, teaching young people who strive for antipollution that they use the idealist demand equally to defy society. All these idealists who want to show that society is
wrong, do not look at what they are doing to their teachers, their parents, everyone who
does not agree with them—which is a trait that is part of the psychotic pattern.

How did we come to that? Through a misunderstanding of democracy. People think they
can do anything they want to satisfy themselves and to find themselves. It is the birth
pains of a new society, based on the assumption that everyone is free to do as he pleases
regardless of the consequences. [27, p. 134]

Perhaps this freedom and lack of responsibility is what has made the modern-day
democratic processes so slow and cumbersome. Another ironic and darkly amusing
corollary to this is the statement attributed to Winston Churchill, "Democracy is the
worst kind of political system in existence—except for all of the others."

What is perhaps ominous about Dreikurs's statement is that it emphasizes what
appears to have been promoted, whether unwittingly or not, by the encounter
group movement which swept the country during the last two decades. Much of
this movement is rooted in the existential concept of finding one's "self," which
does not have as its goal any antihumanistic or antisocial connotation. However,
often the results of many encounter groups is that the search of meaning and the,
"Who am I, what am I, where do I fit in society, and in the cosmos?" often degen-
erates into the need to express oneself and learn to show one's "true" feelings.
Whether others understand them or are hurt by them is not terribly important.
Though the encounter group movement is viewed by its creators as a significant
aid in solving many of the ills of society because it reaches larger numbers of
people than an individual therapist could, thus far its results seem to be more in
line with Dreikurs's predictions than with what its founders had hoped.

Ironically, Dreikurs's solution to the problem rests also in the development of
groups, but obviously on a very different basis. He also points out that in his view,
neither the psychiatric nor the psychological profession as they are presently con-
stituted and being trained are equipped to do this task. Perusing some of the current offerings in psychiatry and psychology does support this view. The real task
is to train, not only as many psychologists and psychiatrists and teachers and others in the professional ranks, but paraprofessionals as well. This is not a new idea,
but to many professionals in the field it is not only revolutionary, but frightening.

I will give you an example of the development professional resistance. At the University
of Oregon in Eugene, some of my graduate students gave a class in counseling parents
and found that some of the parents, without any academic training, were more effective
in influencing other parents than were professionals. So they made an experiment, inviting three or four of the parents to participate in class. Unfortunately, to the psychologist,
this was not acceptable. They stated in masse, "You make up your mind. If you take lay
people in this class, we step out." [27, p. 145]

However, much as a result of Dreikurs's urging in this regard in 1972, the North
American Society of Adlerian Psychology abandoned the two-tiered structure of

its membership. The description of lay and professional members was abolished. Despite some early resistance from the professional members, a significant growth, not only in membership in the Society, has occurred since then. There was, of course, resistance to this concept on the grounds that it would create an inadequately trained group of nonprofessionals. However, local groups were invited to set their own standards for competence in the field. So far, few of even the most vehement critics of this move have dropped out of the Society, and the number of licensed and credentialed as well as degree-earning professionals in the Society have greatly increased.

Unfortunately, even this growth has not made much of an impact, considering the imminent problems that modern society faces, many of which are the result of the breakdown in masculine authority that Adler and Dreikurs prophesied. Discussion will be held on some of these problems and their possible solutions in a later chapter.

Chapter Seven

Self-Actualization and Social Interest

Adler's concept of social interest is one that superficially seems to be quite simple and easy to comprehend, and yet in reality is extraordinarily complex and not very well understood outside of Adlerian circles today.

Adler first coined the term *Gemeinschaftsgefühl* to denote what he felt was an attitude the individual needed to possess in achieving satisfactory relationships with others. In defining what he called the "communal life," he stated,

In addition to regarding an individual life as a unity, we must also take it together with its contexts of social relations. Thus, when children are first born, they are weak and their weakness makes it necessary for persons to care for them. The style or pattern of a child's life cannot be understood without reference to the persons who look after him and who make up for his inferiority. The child has interlocking relations with the mother and family which could never be understood if we confined our analysis to the periphery of the child's physical being in space. The individuality of the child cuts across his physical individuality and involves a whole context of social relations. [18, p. 127]

In further clarifying this he added,

One of the basic facts of the advancement of our understanding of human nature is that we must regard the inherited rules of the game of the group as these emerge within the limited organization of the human body and its achievement—as if they were an absolute truth. We are able to approach this truth only slowly, and usually only after mistakes and errors have been overcome. [18, p. 128]

To understand this, we must realize that what Adler meant by the "absolute truth," was to be interpreted as to how the individual must respond to the demands of this "communal life" in which he exists. As Ansbacher pointed out, the term "absolute truth" was not to be taken at face value:

When Adler calls the fact of the social embeddedness of the individual the absolute truth, this is not to be taken in the literal sense of the term absolute. Adler was a positivistic idealist, rather than a transcendental idealist. Thus, by the absolute truth he meant something like the following: "Since we do not have any absolute answers and since nevertheless we have a need for certainty to guide our conduct, the most useful fiction or working hypothesis is to consider the iron logic of the communal life of man as if it were the absolute truth." Adler's justification for this fiction was his clinical observation that all problem cases, from neuroses and psychoses to criminality, have in common their failure to abide by this "absolute truth." [18, p. 128–129]

Although these demands differ from culture to culture, but obviously still involve certain fundamental truths which transcend culture, the most fundamental of these might be considered as the need of entirety regardless of whether this feeling is reciprocated or not. It was also Adler's belief that few of us could function with any degree of success in any society without some degree of social interest. Also, to him the greater our development of this attitude, the more successful we became as human beings.

THE THREE LIFE TASKS

How is social interest evaluated? In describing this Adler divided the social responsibilities of the individual into what he termed the "three life tasks," namely occupation, friendship or social relationships in general, and love. The degree of success the individual manifested in each of these three areas was at least, to a considerable extent, a method by which the success of the person's relationship with others could be judged. He thought it was necessary for the individual to be successful in all three areas to be considered truly psychologically healthy. Adler also suggested an ascending order of difficulty among the three, with occupation as the least and love as the most difficult to achieve. The criteria for evaluating would be the degree of closeness or distance, as the case may be, that the individual maintains between himself and his fellows.

Occupation

Even such a menial task as a janitor or farm laborer is as much a social necessity as those of a physicist, doctor, or engineer. Accordingly, no one *should* be valued over any other (although sadly, this is not the case). However, it is still possible for an individual to be successful in an occupation without having either friendship or close ties of love with other individuals.

Friendship

Up one rung on the ladder, a person may have relatively close friendships, although this requires more closeness and willingness to relate and share than in fulfilling an occupation.

Love

It is interesting that though the nature of the relationships in the first two areas have not materially changed since Adler first formulated them, there has been a significant alteration in our understanding of the character of the relationship of love—particularly in those societies which have evolved to the highest degrees of personal and individual freedom. Perhaps the most important of these changes is that the closeness and intimacy of a love relationship between two individuals does not necessarily depend on marriage—or for that matter, the sex of the individuals involved. Although there is much controversy between various points of view in this area, to many, the institution of heterosexual marriage is still seen as a stabilizing influence and a legal procedure, within which the rights of the children are more fully protected than in a nonmarriage relationship. Until recently this was considered in most Western cultures to be the highest form of communal association. Even though legal sanction is not yet available, there appears to be little doubt that eventually marriage among homosexuals may also be permitted by society. There are still those who argue that a love relationship among individuals without marriage is, in a real sense, an avoidance of the highest level of commitment. Perhaps this may be true, but the social mores and practices of our society, particularly in America and other Western countries, are changing so rapidly that one cannot truly say that an institution such as marriage is necessary for two people to achieve the highest state of intimacy and love.

Though all forms of love do require a willingness to share and risk hurt through closeness, it is not difficult to comprehend that true intimacy between adults, particularly involving sexual relationships, is probably the most difficult to achieve. If the love songs of the poets through the ages are any measure, perhaps the rewards of such a union may as well be the most profound. Though changes in our society seem to have broadened the definition of love beyond how Adler defined it, his conception of the attitude necessary to achieve this transcendent state are still relevant today.

SELF-ACTUALIZATION

It is ironic to note that Adler's ideas on social interest were never widely understood and might have been largely forgotten, even among practicing Adlerians today, had it not been for a monumental study on what he called "self-actualization," done by Abraham Maslow in the late 1940s [54]. Even though Maslow himself admitted the inadequacies of his study, which was not done by utilizing any of the conventional standards of statistical measurements that are employed in research today, he equally acknowledged the heavy contribution Adler's ideas had made to his thinking. The concept of self-actualization, as Maslow described it, has come to be one of the most widely accepted measures of what could be called "psychological health" or the opposite end of the scale as contrasted with "neurosis, criminality, or psychosis." In his research, Maslow made the first comprehensive and intensive effort to study and identify the characteristic of individuals with what he called the "optimum" level of psychological health. It is important to note that he avoided the word "adjustment," a term that psychologists and psychiatrists used for many years to denote those who could function more efficiently in society than those who could not. Unfortunately, adjustment also denotes conformity—so that if the society in which you live believes implicitly that blacks and Jews are inferior to Aryan whites, adjustment to that particular mode of thinking in Nazi Germany, for example, might have made one popular—but *not* psychologically healthy. In fact, many of the subjects whom Maslow called self-actualized were often, to a considerable degree, nonconformists to the general rules of their own contemporary society.

Characteristics of Self-Actualizing Persons

Maslow also acknowledged that all his subjects possessed a high degree of social interest, specifically in the way Adler described it. When one studies the characteristics of the individuals Maslow considered self-actualized, much of their behavior toward others, even those whom they considered disagreeable, prejudiced or downright nasty, was characterized by a degree of compassion and caring that could rarely be found among the general population. All of them, to one degree or another, were involved in projects which were concerned primarily with betterment of the lot of others. All of them were more problem-centered than self-centered, which conforms strongly with what Adler described as the "psychology of use rather than possession." It is more what a person did with his assets than how he talked about them or how they were described. They were consistently more accurate in their perception of reality, which in essence means that their observations of relationships with people, political attitudes, and the ability to sense the genuine individual from the fraud, was much more highly developed than in others. They were also more accepting of the limitations of their own physical being and the nature of the process by which democratic and totalitarian societies functioned.

They were also overwhelmingly nonviolent in character, but were still able to perceive that in some situations, violence could not be avoided when the needs of the majority were being subverted by the minority. One of the most notable proponents of this view was Albert Einstein, who was considered by Maslow as one of the self-actualized subjects in his study. Yet it was Einstein who wrote the memorable personal letter to Franklin D. Roosevelt during World War II, in which he urged the United States develop the atomic bomb before the Nazis could perfect their experiments on it. This letter was probably the final most important reason that convinced Roosevelt to commit more than $2 billion and the scientists to push the project to its successful conclusion. There may be those who wish that such a letter might never have been written, but subsequent revelations after the war at least verify Einstein's judgment. He was correct in asserting the Germans were only a few months behind us.

The Scope of Self-Actualization

Although Maslow discovered the number of individuals whom he could truly consider to be self-actualized was distressingly small, even finding those who fulfilled his conception of self-actualization was a more laborious and demanding process than he had envisioned. In fact, it was necessary in the later stages of his study to resort to historical data about people who had lived many years before. He also added to his group some whom he felt certain appeared to fall short, but possessed many, if not all, of the characteristics of those whom he identified as self-actualizing.

In Maslow's later book *Motivation and Personality* [53], he also presented a newer concept of a presumed "hierarchy of human needs," ranging from the lowest level, the necessity for simple, elemental, and fundamental life resources such as air, water, food, and comfort, to the highest need, which he considered to be self-actualization. In his view, the higher level needs could only be achieved after the more primitive biological drives had been satisfied. Though there have been disagreements with the order in which he placed some in his hierarchy, it has also become, to a considerable extent, a standard by which psychological health is measured today.

Essentially, Maslow recognized that self-actualizing people, being human, are not immune from the inner problems which beset all of us—self-doubt, worries, prejudices, and at times, a rather extraordinary ruthlessness toward other people. They display these characteristics less often than others and, as can be seen by those who study Maslow, he went considerably beyond Adler in his interpretation of *Gemeinschaftsgefühl*, though it still remains at the core of his description of self-actualizing people.

Not only is this foundation automatically (and universally) supplied *all* SA's by their intrinsic dynamics (so that in at least this respect fully developed human nature may be universal and cross-cultural); other determiners are supplied as well by these same dynamics. Among these are:

(a) his peculiarly comfortable relationships with reality,

(b) his *Gemeinschaftsgefühl*,

(c) his basically satisfied condition from which flow, as epiphanymena, various consequences of surplus of wealth, over-flowing abundance, and

(d) his characteristic relations to means and ends, etc.

One most important consequence of this attitude toward the world—as well as a validation of it—is the fact that conflict and struggle, ambivalence and uncertainty over choice, lessen or disappear in many areas of life. Apparently, morality is largely an epiphenomenon of non-acceptance or dissatisfaction. Many "problems" are seen to be gratuitous and fade out of the existence in the atmosphere of pagan acceptance.

The pursuit of finding more profound levels has suggested to the writer that much else of what passes for morals, ethics and values may be the gratuitous epiphenomena of the pervasive psychopathology of the "average." Many conflicts, frustrations and threats (which force the kind of choice in which value is expressed), evaporate or resolve for the self-actualizing person in the same way as do, let us say, conflicts over dancing. For him, the seemingly irreconcilable battle of the sexes becomes no conflict at all, but rather a delightful collaboration. The "antagonistic" interests of adults and children turn out to be not so antagonistic after all. [53, p. 14]

Here one might be inclined to view Maslow's statement in conformance with the present day existential philosophy of being one's self regardless of the outcome. One of what appears to be the sought-for outcomes of the encounter group movement which became highly developed in later years, particularly in the United States, is the belief that an essential characteristic of being one's self is the freedom to express one's fear, anger, or hostility, regardless of what the consequences may be to others. This can be considered a pendulum shift away from the excessive, theological, and to some extent psychological morality of the past that was espoused by many, and in which others have often misinterpreted Adler's concept of social interest to mean the contrary. According to Maslow, the self-actualizing person never goes out of his way to harm someone. If he does, it is accidental or in pursuit of the greater good for others. Fundamental conflicts in relationships may seem less important to him than to others, but never in situations where people are hurt by this. On the other hand, neither does the self-actualizing person feel obligated to help others. To him the highest rewards in life generally revolve around this kind of pursuit. The degree of social interest that the individual manifests can be evaluated by determining how much of what he did helped or hurt people, and in the pursuit of satisfaction how much he enjoys what he is doing. Perhaps the most important values that can be achieved from studying both Adler and Maslow are that Maslow has helped us to better define the direction in which we can develop ourselves. Adler has provided us with a theory, as well as techniques, by which any or all of us, if we practice it, can achieve self-actualization if we wish.

Chapter Eight

Major Factors That Influence the Personality Development of the Child

HEREDITY VERSUS ENVIRONMENT

There has perhaps been no fiercer battle waged in all of psychology during this century than that relating to the possible influence of the individual's heredity versus his environment on his behavior. However, the core of the controversy seems to have centered mostly around the development of intelligence. In the days of Freud, Binet, and William MacDougall near the turn of the century, the fundamental basis of personality traits were considered instinctual, although it was agreed that the environment did play a role in altering or at least influencing this growth. In most psychological thinking during subsequent years, instinct has gradually been considered to have only a relatively minor role in personality development, although since the emergence of the newest twin studies, a great deal of controversy still exists regarding intelligence. The conflict between the hereditarian and the environmentalist views over the basis of intelligence is still far from being resolved. The pendulum has seen some remarkable swings from the extreme instinctual views of MacDougall to those of the behaviorist John B. Watson as early as 1921. Watson at one time is alleged to have asserted quite flatly that he could take any normal, healthy infant regardless of sex or race and, given proper environment, transform him into any professional occupation he chose, or for that matter, even make a genius of him.

We have now seen the pendulum swing back as early as the 1970s in the bold statements of William B. Shockley [63] and Arthur Jensen [50]. The latter concluded, as a result of his extensive studies of lower-class black and white children with the use of conventional intelligence tests, that blacks were constitutionally inferior to whites in intellectual capacity. Shockley for a time toured the country lecturing extensively about his theory of "sperm banks" and what amounts to "selective breeding" to increase the intelligence level of the race, as he put it. These views have been disputed by other recent studies which have asserted that special environmental stimulation can improve the I.Q. level of any child as much as 20 to 40 points, regardless of race or background. Although the environmentalist view of intelligence appears to be more pronounced now, and certainly a great deal more since MacDougall, if one is to listen to Shockley and Jensen and their followers, the issue is still far from resolved. Additional research has also revealed that lower-class black children score higher in I.Q. tests which were administered by black teachers than those administered by white.

ADLER'S EARLY VIEWS

What is interesting and notable about Adler in his contribution to this issue is that though his first studies dealt to a great degree with the biological basis for certain types of physical inferiorities, he rejected the hereditary notion of the basis of personality as early as 1929, when he stated the following:

The idea of a congenital origin of character is untenable because, for the formation of psychic character in whatever part thereof may be congenital is metamorphesic under the influence of a guiding ideal until this idea is satisfied. [8, p. 38]

He also strongly condemned the attitudes he felt to be overly prevalent in the schools of that day—ideas that tended to blame on heredity much of the faults of a child's inability to learn.

Of all the mistakes made in education, the belief in hereditarian limits to development is the worst. It gives teachers and parents an opportunity to explain away their errors and diminish their efforts. They can be freed from the responsibility of their influence over the children. Every attempt to avoid responsibility should be opposed. If an educator really attributed the whole development of character and intelligence to heredity, I do not see how he could possibly hope to accomplish anything in his profession. If, on the other hand, he sees that his own attitude and exertions influence the children, he cannot find an escape from responsibility in views of inheritance. [14, p. 107]

Adler was also critical of the use of conventional types of intelligence tests which, if scores were not high, tended from his point of view to influence teachers to set limits on a child's development. At the same time, he was careful to point out that the "inner environment," as he called it, which consists of all the physical characteristics that we have inherited, does exercise a profound influence on the attitudes any given child or adult might develop in his growth process. Though Adler emphasized that the "outer environment," with all of its pressures, limitations, and opportunities, was undoubtedly the more powerful of the two (excepting in such cases where a biological inferiority was so great that the child could not be normal in intelligence), he saw personality and intelligence as an interaction between the two. Of course, the most important factor he considered was the child's attitude toward both, and how they interacted with one another in the process of his growing and comparisons between himself and others in his environment. It was these *conclusions* that the child drew from all this that Adler felt determined the direction of his development.

Mind–Body Correlations

It is interesting to note that Adler at that time also called attention to a phenomenon which has puzzled philosophers, writers, and even psychologists for ages, and which precipitated a series of rather extensive studies, the results of which unfortunately have been largely forgotten today. A number of thinkers had noted that there seemed to be a correlation between individuals with a certain body type and their personalities. Such a phenomenon was noted more than four hundred years ago by Shakespeare (who may have been the greatest psychologist of them all). In his play of the same name, Julius Caesar says, "Let me have men about me that are fat; /Sleek-headed men and such as sleep o' nights. /Yond Cassius has a lean and hungry look; /He thinks too much: Such men are dangerous!" [I. ii: 191–194].

In the early 1920s a German psychologist named Kretschmer described certain individuals with body types who, he believed, tended toward obesity and who also appeared to possess somewhat better functioning digestive organs than others. To them, Kretschmer assigned such personality traits as joviality, pleasantness, and friendliness. The opposites in his proposals were the tall, slender, asthenic individuals such as Cassius described by Caesar might have been, who he asserted tended to be reserved, introspective, and if they were affected with severe mental difficulties, often became schizophrenic. A later American researcher, G. M. Sheldon [64], made an intensive study of young college-age males, loosely based on Kretschmer's ideas, which he categorized in three separate body types that he called endomorphic, mesomorphic, and ectomorphic. Sheldon's conclusions, as the result of extensive photographic examinations and psychological testing, was that these groups also tended personality-wise to fit the characteristic that Kretschmer had originally assigned them with mesomorphic, or the middle group between the two extremes, as being the vigorous, muscular, somewhat hyperactive person, which Sheldon called the "athletic" type. Sheldon also did a later study which demonstrated that most juvenile delinquents in the sample he studied tended to fall into the mesomorphic group, but to also have facial characteristics that were considered distasteful when being viewed by other groups of college students. Sheldon also attempted to commence a similar study at the University of Washington, using female subjects; but when the university officials discovered that he intended to use nude photos of his subjects for comparisons, as he had done with males, the study was quickly aborted. Of course, Kretschmer and Sheldon both noted that there were many mixed types whose characteristics were not as clear. Also, unfortunately, their conclusions were very much the same— that to them it was the body type that determined the personality. Even though Sheldon's findings have been corroborated by studies done with men and women in England, they were largely discredited because of a very small amount of research here in the United States which appeared to demonstrate different results.

A Different Interpretation

If one were to view these studies from an Adlerian viewpoint, a good deal of the relationships suggested by Kretschmer and Sheldon would appear to make more sense. However, the personality characteristics are the *result* of the person's view of his body. If one has a body relatively free of organ imperfections, as it appeared Sheldon's endomorphic subjects did, there would at least be a tendency for them to look upon life more favorably than, for example, Sheldon's ectomorphic, whom he found generally to suffer respiratory difficulties, be more sensitive to pain, and usually developed their physical coordination later than others.

Sociological Alterations

It is interesting, however, to note that the cultural changes in our attitudes to- ward the "jolly fat man," as Kretschmer called him, have tended to alter consider- ably in interpretations of this particular body–mind correlation as far as psychology was concerned. Though Sheldon's endomorphic subjects were gen- erally more obese than were the other two extremes, they did not tend toward ex- cessive weight as did Kretschmer's. If one were to project Sheldon's studies to today's American culture, probably the individual most idealized, at least among youth, might be the mesomorphic or the athlete, and the fashion model or cinema star if the subject were a woman. The "jolly fat man" no longer exists as a desir- able type, but rather an individual who has almost become the object of derision and pity. So again, it would appear that the most powerful determining factor in self-attitudes would not be how a person's body functioned, but *how he felt about what others think of him*. A correlative study done once on a group of weight lifters who spent many hours developing the huge, bulging muscles that they dis- played revealed that a significant majority of these men were found to have se- vere doubts about their masculinity. The weight lifting programs they adhered to appeared to be designed to make sure no one else had similar doubts.

So it can be seen that if we view the body–mind correlation as an interactive process, it is also strongly and intimately related to the interaction between the individual and those around him. Perhaps it can then be assumed that it is not how well or poorly the body functions or even how well or poorly others think of the individual's body and its functioning, but *how the individual sees himself and what he believes others think about his appearance and bodily function*.

Changes in Women

Again, the application of today's cultural standards on the physical appearance of women might not show much difference as far as body functioning was concerned than men, but certainly a much greater difference exists in the cultural attitude about the physical appearance of a woman. Two hundred years ago, a woman who was slim was not considered as beautiful as one who was voluptuous, particularly as portrayed by painters such as Rembrandt, whose figures tended toward obesity. Ironically, this may have been largely because most overweight people of that day were among the few who had enough to eat. Today, the young overweight woman is far more scorned than the overweight man. So the ideal of the beautiful, athletic woman seems to resemble the same ideal as that for a man. These two factors alone may have almost more to do with the personality development of young men and women in the Western world than anything else. Perhaps to sum up what the Adlerian interpretation means as applied to Kretschmer's and Sheldon's findings, it appears that if we see ourselves as too fat, too thin, too tall, too short, not handsome, or not pretty enough, the resulting attitudes can lead to overcompensations, some of which are often very damaging to our self-image, not to mention the social consequences for others.

THE OUTER ENVIRONMENT: PARENTAL INFLUENCES

Adler was quite explicit in his descriptions of the importance of family influences on the child, particularly those of the mother.

This connection is so intimate and far reaching that we are never able in later years to point to any characteristic as the effect of heredity. Every tendency which might be inherited has been adapted, trained, educated and made over again by the mother. Her skill or lack of skill will influence all the child's potentiality. We mean nothing else by a mother's skill than her ability to cooperate with her child and to win the child's cooperation with her. [4, p. 167]

We might add that in today's society, such a relationship does not necessarily have to be that of the mother. Though it might happen rarely, it is certainly conceivable that the father could play a similar role in the early development of an infant child. What is critically important here, of course, is the relationship that the parents develop with the child. Of course, in Adler's day this was considered almost solely the mother's role.

The Role of Women in Society

Despite this, Adler was one of the earliest to point out the difficulties women encountered, even around the turn of the century, in accepting this role because society accorded it such little value. Unfortunately in the ensuing years, the attitude of society toward the mother's role has changed very little. As a consequence, though in Western societies, women gradually are achieving greater rights and more equality, their movement in this effort has been away from home and more into the direction of a career in competition with men. However, it is true that there are many women today who appear to have managed to combine both roles successfully. The significant effects of this development are dealt with further in another chapter.

What Adler did see most clearly is that it was the *attitude* the mother or mother-substitute developed toward the infant immediately after birth that was of the most importance.

In all her activities, we can see her attitude. Whenever she picks the baby up, carries him, speaks to him, bathes him, feeds him, she has the opportunity to connect him with herself. If she is not trained in her task or interested in him she will be clumsy and the baby will resist. If she has never learned how to bathe a child, he may find bathing an unpleasant experience. Instead of being in connection with her, he will try to get rid of her. She must be skillful in the way she puts her baby to bed. All of her movements and the noises she makes must be skillful in watching him or leaving him alone. At every occasion she is providing an opportunity for the child to like or dislike her, to cooperate or reject cooperation. [4, p. 168]

What is interesting about these statements is that Adler does not once mention the word "love" in this paragraph. A rather startling presumption could be made here that goes against literally millions of words written about the need for the mother to "love" the child. Only the mother's attitude, which Adler interprets as concern for the child's welfare, and what she then does about it, appear to be the critical elements.

A concerned stranger who might be required by some circumstances to be the sole individual responsible for the care of the child and providing proper food could be found and undoubtedly could quite adequately teach a child cooperation. There would seem to be little doubt that from this relationship, if it lasted for any length of time, that love could develop. And of course, the studies which have dealt extensively with this subject have talked about mothering, cuddling, stroking, talking to the child, in addition to feeding and changing him. The process itself is the critical element.

Harlow's Findings

The classic researches on infant Rhesus monkeys by Harry Harlow [44] reinforces this important premise. In his earlier studies, the newborn monkeys who had been taken from their real mothers at birth rejected the wire enclosed mother substitute for the cloth one, even though the wire mother fed them and the cloth one did not. In either case, when the monkeys matured, they showed a singular inability to function sexually or to care for their own infants if any were born. But in Harlow's later experiments, he put newborn Rhesus monkeys in pairs and they were only fed and left to their own devices. In nearly all cases when these monkeys matured, they were able to carry on normal sexual and mothering functions themselves.

In any event, whoever provides these essential services to the newborn infant, if he is deprived of adequate affection he will not develop physically as well as mentally, even if adequately fed and clothed. Perhaps unfortunately for the feminists in today's society, the mother is still expected to take on the major role and responsibility in child-rearing; and of course, if the child is wanted at all, the fact that the child comes from her womb does serve to strengthen the bond between them. It is, however, rather surprising that hospital routines have been altered in the last twenty years to the degree that the child, unless premature or severely ill, is given to the mother almost immediately after birth. The father's role, though perhaps not enough, has begun to change in this respect as well. He is allowed, but not necessarily expected, to play a larger role in the care and nurturing of the child. What many fathers today do not realize is that this can be a deeply satisfying and rewarding experience. It may even compensate to some degree for the fact that he is no longer regarded as the boss—or at least if he is at all, only up to a certain point.

Infant Care Is Learned

It is also important to understand that most of what has to be done to properly rear an infant, or a child of any age, can be taught. Particularly under the influence of Dreikurs, many parent study groups, education classes, and family counseling centers have been established to help parents with this vital challenge. Here in the United States and also many Western European nations, Adlerian principles of child-rearing provide clear, concise methods of helping parents cope with increasingly complex relationships that have developed in this technological age. This is especially important today, because of the weakening of the family as a nuclear unit, and the myriad pressures from the outside world which tend to disrupt normal family relationships.

FAMILY PATTERNS

In addition to the specific things parents do for and to their children during the early years, the relationship between the parents, and the types of occupations and creative skills one or more parent might possess, has an important influence on the development of the child. If either parent is talented artistically, athletically, or in any capacity which affords recognition in our society, children will attempt to emulate these talents or develop those which are close enough to obtain similar recognition. Parents usually encourage such talents, but often there can be difficulties for other children in a given family if one child develops a superior skill than others in a given area.

Paternal Domination

There can also be negative patterns. Studies have shown that excessively domineering parents tend to inhibit independence in their children, although the type of domination, either masculine or feminine, may exert considerably different influences on the children. In the more patriarchal societies, children of an excessively domineering father often develop ways of attempting to please him and at the same time avoid him when he is angry or excessively bossy. Often boys in such a family attempt to repeat such patterns with their own children. In the more equalitarian societies, excessive masculine dominance by the father more often produces rebellion, particularly among boys. Sometimes this can develop into juvenile delinquency.

Maternal Domination

This is often accomplished by the mother holding herself up as the most efficient member of the household and belittling the efforts of the children to imitate her. Such an attitude can be devastating for girls. It robs them of their feelings of self-worth in any capacity that mother excels. Boys are less affected because they are usually not supposed to excel in the traits such as helping around the house or getting good grades. In such families, it is usually one parent who is dominating and the other submissive.

Submissive and Overprotective Parents

In families where both parents are submissive, the children often tend to grow up bossy, domineering, and want to make their own rules. There are many variations and the other two extremes of attitude are rejection and overprotection. Delinquency is often the result of rejection of one or both parents, with the greatest extreme being the psychopathic personality. Children who come from extremely overprotective homes tend to be timid and unsure of themselves. They have great difficulty in making independent decisions of their own.

The Results of Deprivation

To the list of family patterns we must also add those which are the product of deprivation. Parents who rear children in a ghetto environment where there is little opportunity for proper education or advancement have enormous disadvantages. They themselves often possess few saleable skills and are often so overwhelmed with the necessity of sheer survival that they are unable to provide their children with sufficient affection or intellectual stimulation to allow them to grow normally. Sadly enough, in the midst of the enormous affluence of American society, there are whole generations of children who grow up in what to them is a hostile or largely indifferent world. At rate intervals, under the influence of a caring teacher, counselor, or friend, a few of these children are rescued before it is too late. Though the methods are there, unfortunately ghetto inhabitants are often so discouraged that they rarely avail themselves of them. But, even in an extremely deprived environment, there are still some children who simply break out of this on their own, often without any outside help, and become successful, loving human beings.

Changes in Family Patterns

It must be remembered that these patterns were established some time ago and were related primarily to families that were not materially separated by divorce, death, or remarriage of one or another parent. It is obvious that whenever any new member enters a given family, there is a significant change in interaction among all the family members. It is also obvious that with a separation or divorce, or the death of a parent, the family pattern is altered. The parental pattern also will change more if the parent who retains the custody of the child develops a new relationship with a different person or remarries. Today, in an overwhelming number of instances, the mother secures custody of the child, then carries what elements of the pattern she has learned into a new relationship. The implications here would seem then to be that in most family circumstances, the mother continues to exert the greatest influence on the child—which is to considerable extent almost the opposite of what has occurred in earlier masculine-dominated societies. It is also important to understand that whatever the change in the family pattern, it is possible for a single parent to successfully rear children alone.

BIRTH ORDER AND ITS INFLUENCES ON THE CHILD

Adler was the first of the major psychologists in this century to emphasize the significant influences that birth order plays in the personality development of the child. Many of his predictions on the types of personalities that would on the average emerge as a result of birth order (with some other factors being noted) have been strongly supported by current research, at least among children in certain ordinal positions. However, in view of the fact that there can only be truly five clear-cut positions, which also change with the advent of new family members, the great majority of the innumerable studies that have been conducted on birth order seem to be concentrated on the first and second positions—or firstborns versus those born later—and predominately on the first. Of the firstborn, for statistical purposes, there are two categories: only children, and first children with one or more younger siblings. Beyond that would be the second child in a two child family who is also the youngest; also, the youngest in a large family. The fifth and rather clear-cut position would be that of a middle child in a three child family. Beyond that single category, in dealing with middle children, so many factors enter the situation as to make accurate statistical research extremely difficult.

Adler was careful to point out that it was the *situation* in which the child found himself and his interpretation of it that influenced his development, not the actual position as such. Again, the overwhelming motivation here that appears to impel children to compete against one another is the attention of the parents. They will, of course, try to attain the parents's recognition favorably at first. If this is not possible, negative attention will lead the first child to try and maintain the power he held before the displacement, and the second child will try to "steal" it.

For example, the characteristics that appeared to have been most prized by the NASA leaders who picked twenty out of twenty-two firstborns for the initial group of astronauts were responsibility, a considerable degree of cooperation, and the ability to carry out orders promptly, efficiently, and correctly. Apparently, the daring "fly boys" who became fighter pilots during World Wars I and II were certainly not the type of individuals that NASA would have chosen to carry out the moon landings.

Though emphasizing intelligence rather than personality development, a corollary to this is a recent study done on a massive Dutch population numbering several hundred thousand, who were all given an English I.Q. test called Raven's Progressive Matrices, which considered ordinal position in the family as a variable. The mean I.Q. scores of the population sampled revealed that firstborn (with other siblings) in these groups achieved the highest scores, followed closely by only children. Later-born children other than the youngest were third in the ranking, followed by youngests, who scored the lowest. Though the mean scores were in a very narrow range, the very large size of the sample indicated differences that were considered significant by the researchers. This study suggests that intelligence and personality may be to some extent related. Oldest and only children, being adult-oriented and introspective, tend to develop themselves more intellectually, as Adler had proposed, than later borns. The "super-duper baby," as Adler portrays the youngest, also may perceive less of a necessity to compete with older siblings in intellectual pursuits, very often being the most pampered of all the children, particularly in large families.

Later Borns

The practice of lumping most of research studies made tells us much about the traits of firstborns. But it only suggests that later borns are different. A book by Frank Sulloway, *Born to Rebel* [71], offers some significant research that suggests overwhelmingly that later borns are more rebellious and less dominating than firstborns, but beyond this a great variation in personality types is revealed from his writings. Although Sulloway gives a great many historical examples of how positions other than firstborn develop themselves, he gives little statistical verification as to how the influence of these other positions helps to shape their personality development. Adler's views on some of the other positions may be helpful in giving us some insight into differences between the individual children in a given family.

The Second Child

Adler once called the second born, "the steam engine child." Today, he might be labeled the "jet-propelled child." Essentially, the attempt of the second born appears to be to try to "catch up" with the oldest and, if possible, overtake him, at least as far as soliciting parental favoritism is concerned. This rarely happens however, and it is the reason why second children are much more likely to take an opposite, rather than similar direction of development than that of the first child. Some research has indicated that seconds are likely to be more flexible— change sometimes operates to their advantage, but it nearly always is considered as destructive by the oldest. Second children appear to be generally more creative but less likely to follow through on responsibilities than firstborns. If the first child fails to exploit a trait which the parents prize, the second child very often moves into exploit this "vacuum."

The advent of a third child usually appears to place more pressure on the second than on the first. Very often if this middle child is discouraged and feels that he does not have a place, his biggest problem is indecision. Should he be responsible or be the baby?

The Youngest Child

The youngest, particularly in families of three children or more, finds himself in a totally different situation than that of the others. He is most often babied, pampered by the rest, and less is expected of him. Very often however, he has the feeling that no one pays any attention to what he says because there are too many spokesmen ahead of him. If a family occupational pattern is broken, the youngest appears to be the most likely to break it. There is also some newer research which suggests that in many instances the youngest boy, particularly in poorer families, tends to have more problems in school, particularly in academic areas.

Middle Children in Large Families

Both Adler and Dreikurs have stressed that the only conclusions that can be safely drawn regarding children in these positions are that children next to each other in sequence are more likely to have opposite personality characteristic than those with one or more children in intervening positions. For example, if a first and second child are most opposite in personality traits, the third child may be more like the first, particularly if there is a fourth or more children in the family. And, of course, distances in age and sex of each child will, in turn, alter these patterns.

Other Influences

In addition to those already mentioned, other factors may have much to do with the personality development of any child in a given family. A special talent or handicap of a given child can create problems for others. A premature death in the family or removal or addition of any child or adult in the family group can alter the interaction, and to some degree, the personality development of the rest. These are added reasons why Adler's views and even research results may be treated with caution in dealing with *any* child.

SULLOWAY'S FINDINGS

As mentioned, Sulloway's researches did not deal extensively with other positions except as specifically compared to firstborns; however, his book is replete with descriptions of the behavior of subjects, mostly famous historical figures, of differing positions with conclusions about their behavior often in agreement with Adler. He also devotes one chapter to positions of famous women in history whose patterns were often similar to those of men, though usually their traits of dominance and rebellion tended to be more within cultural norms than with males.

Despite the limitations of his research, particularly in his choice of subjects not reflecting cultural mores, Sulloway's monumental work should go a long way in exploding the myth that ordinal position plays no role in personality development. Adler, as well as his followers up until today, have successfully utilized ordinal positions as a means of diagnosis almost since the beginning of his discoveries.

There appears little doubt that ordinal position plays a powerful role in determining personality development, but even Sulloway admits it can only be revealed in concert with other factors.

Though Sulloway's findings came nearly seventy years after Adler's observations, as far as they go, his results are striking. Despite this, Sulloway devotes less than a full page to Adler's discoveries and concluded his statement by saying "Adler's hypothesis can accommodate itself to almost any psychological outcome. Adler's firstborns can be conservative or rebellious, Adlerian later borns can be competitive or lazy. To be useful, these hypotheses need to be stated in ways that are refutable" [71, p. 51]. Sulloway gives no explanation as to how he arrived at this conclusion. By trying so obviously to belittle Adler's findings, to some degree Sulloway appears to have become the victim of his own refutable hypothesis. By failing to isolate Adler's only children in his firstborn samples, and by lumping all others under the rubric of "later borns," Sulloway has come close to contradicting some of his own theories. Despite this, even in ignoring Adler's detailed description of the differences between only children, oldest children, second children, and youngest children, Sulloway's hypotheses to a considerable extent are rescued by his own results.

Birth Order Studies

In surveying the vast body of research on birth order, Sulloway isolated 196 studies which he considered as meeting the social class and family size criteria, which, in his opinion, made the studies more valid. In this group he found seventy-two that showed significant differences in personality traits between firstborns and later borns. By a technique he calls "meta analysis" (the nature of which he did not describe), he concludes there are sufficient numbers of subjects in those studies to show significant findings. As a result of this analysis, he concludes firstborns are found to be "aggressive, ambitious, jealous and conservative" [71, p. 79]. When we compare these traits with those described by Adler, there are impressive similarities, even though the language is somewhat different. Indeed, in Adler's descriptions regarding firstborns, we have his statement about their "desire for and respect for authority. Aggression and ambition would also appear to relate to the drive for dominance." In his chart of statistical findings, Sulloway's list mentions, as does Adler about oldest, that firstborns tend more toward neuroticism than later borns, and both agree on a universal trait for firstborns—conservatism. Rather interestingly, Sulloway credits most of the "why" in his thesis to the natural selection teachings of Charles Darwin, though there is no evidence given that Darwin was interested in the subject of human birth order at all.

Possibly one of the reasons Sulloway's findings on firstborns are so significant is that there were comparatively few only children in his samples. He does, however, recognize that sex differences play a considerable role in personality development and also supports the idea that the close spacing in age between siblings tends to exacerbate personality differences among them, as did Adler before him.

An example of how family structure can be easily determined by analysis of the relationship between the children in their various positions and with their parents is given in a remarkable family interview that Dreikurs gave in Oregon in the summer of 1961.

The case involved a family consisting of the mother, father, and seven children, ages twenty to six. The mother, Mrs. M., had come to one of the Family Centers in Eugene some months before because of the poor relationship between the father and older children. According to Mrs. M., Mr. M. was very dogmatic, chauvinistic, and authoritarian; he disciplined the older girls severely, having beaten them a number of times. As a result of counseling over a period of several months, the situation had eased somewhat, and the beatings had stopped. For a while, Mrs. M. tried to handle things on her own, but she returned to the center for help again because the first boy had begun to develop behavior disturbances. At this time, the problems seemed to revolve mostly around the second child, a girl of seventeen, and the third child, a girl of thirteen, along with the boy, age eleven. The oldest girl, who was twenty, attended the session, though she was married and not living at home. At first, Dr. Dreikurs talked with the mother alone (Mr. M. did not attend).

DR. DREIKURS: Can you describe what your children are like? How about the oldest?

MRS. M.: She was always the good child and helpful.

DR. DREIKURS: How did she get along with her father?

MRS. M.: Pretty good, though he was mean to her sometimes. Mostly, she tried to stay out of his way.

DR. DREIKURS: What about the second child?

MRS. M.: Well, that was the real problem to start with. She and her father never got along, even from the beginning. She was always rebellious and fought back. Even though he quit beating her, they still yell at each other a lot. We never could control her too much, though she seems to get along all right in school and with her friends.

DR. DREIKURS: Wasn't she the tomboy?

MRS. M.: Oh no, never—it was the thirteen-year-old who was the tomboy.

DR. DREIKURS: (turning to the group) There is something wrong here! This simply doesn't fit. (To Mrs. M.) Is there anything you haven't told me about the family up until now?

MRS. M.: No, I don't think so. Oh yes, wait a minute. There is one thing—there was a boy born after the first girl, Tom Jr.—but he died just a few weeks after birth.

DR. DREIKURS: (to the group) Now, this makes sense! We can see the constellation very clearly. First there was a girl. Of course, father didn't want a girl, but she behaved so he more or less accepted her. Then the boy was born, but he died. The next child was just another girl, and because father wanted a boy so badly, she was rejected. As a result, V., the third girl, became the tomboy and father's favorite. So when your second son was born, there was already a "boy" ahead of him and he had no place to go. So, he became a behavior problem. V.'s problem was that she couldn't compete with a ghost—particularly of a boy who was so much wanted by father. Now, perhaps we should see all of the children.

Though we had not seen the children before, the appearances of the first three girls seemed to conform rather astoundingly to the personality categories the mother had described. O. was blond, rather conservatively dressed but was attractive with no makeup. V. had almost jet black hair, dressed very provocatively, and wore heavy makeup. S. had sandy red hair, freckles, and wore jeans and a plaid shirt. When they were all seated, Dr. Dreikurs again spoke.

Dr. Dreikurs: I see we have a very serious problem here and though I don't have much time to work with you, at least I can tell you what I think you should do. This is particularly for those of you still living at home, and for the sake of the younger children. As I see it, mother has taken over as boss of the house and unless there is some change, things may get a lot worse. My recommendation is to *put Father back as head of the household.* How many of you are willing to do this—or at least try?

He then went around the group, asking each child separately in turn. All of them agreed except V., who said loudly and forcibly, "I wouldn't give that old bastard anything!"

DR. DREIKURS: (to the group) Well, we can see what the problem is here, but perhaps with Dr. Lowe's help, things can be improved.

This is a simplified, but dramatic illustration of the methods Dreikurs used so swiftly and effectively to analyze the factors that, at least in his view, contributed to the problems this family faced. It also reveals how an event such as the birth and death of any child, even at a few weeks, can often drastically alter the personality development of the children who follow. Had this death not happened in this family, perhaps the rejection of the second girl might not have taken place, and she might have taken the tomboy role, rather than the one she chose. Conceivably, this might have had less effect on the third girl who would have been more like the first child, and the boy would have had more of a chance to attain some favoritism from the father.

APPLICATIONS

It has been only recently that other disciplines in family therapy and counseling have begun to pay some attention to the effect of sibling relationships on personality development—this, in spite of the absolute deluge of research studies on ordinal position that have inundated the field, particularly in the last few years. As well, very few teachers and school counselors seem to understand how important it can be to know something about the behavior of the siblings of children with emotional or learning problems. For example, if a child with problems appears to be the only one in the family at that moment who is discouraged, one should look for a possible "star" on either side of him. If all or most of the children appear to be having problems, then more often than not, the parents are disturbed as well. In the former case, the teacher or school counselor may be able to help the parents to remedy the situation, before it becomes too critical; in the latter case, often extensive family counseling is the only answer. Though in every case, there are individual differences in the behavior of any child, being aware of these relationships can be a powerful aid in alleviating problems, whatever they may be.

What Parents Can Do

It must be understood that though parents play a very important role in determining whether or not the types of personality development their children attain result in contributing to constructive rather than destructive behavior, there is little they can do short of outright deprivation to alter these patterns fundamentally. It is also important to realize that regardless of position, if *any* child in a given family can find an area of competency that does not materially conflict with the areas of interest and competence of the other children, and within which he can feel successful, the chances are good that he will have a reasonably positive development. However, understanding the dynamics behind the interrelationship between parents and children in any given family is essential for the professional—or even for the parent as well—to find more positive ways of influencing the children's development.

Chapter Nine

Diagnosing the Lifestyle

This chapter will not be an attempt to cover the entire range of Adlerian diagnostic techniques, but to highlight some of the directions the movement has taken since the initial teachings of Adler and Dreikurs. There have been a number of outstanding clinical manuals and books published on diagnostic procedures; for such publications, consult the Book List published by the Adler School of Professional Psychology in Chicago, and see the Bibliography in this book.

My old friend, therapist, and teacher Lydia Sicher was insistent in repeating this phrase often during the course of her teaching: "Psychology is a science, but psychotherapy is an art." This may serve to explain why the whole field of psychiatric and psychological diagnosis is in such a state of flux today. Psychology has indeed come of age as a science, but few of our practitioners would deny that along side some of the so-called pure sciences such as physics, chemistry, biology, and perhaps even medicine, it is a most imperfect science. Despite its limitations, psychological research has opened up many new vistas both in diagnosing and treating personality disorders. In the last analysis, it is the relationship between the therapist and the patient, or members of any given therapy or encounter group, that determine the extent of attitude change that can occur within a group or therapeutical relationship.

TYPOLOGY IN DIAGNOSIS

We are also witnessing a dramatic swing in the pendulum between psychiatry and psychology. This swing has occurred earlier, but never to the extent as today. We can see a continuum all the way from the original Freudian and Jungian personality "types" to which some segments of psychiatry still stubbornly cling, to a large segment of psychology, led by the Rogerians, and the Gestaltists who do not believe in diagnosis at all—they affirm that the process of therapy is only one of developing a relationship between therapist and patient or between members of a given group. In this view, change occurs from the exploration of the feelings of the participants within the relationship. What has happened in the past, and even what is happening to an individual at the moment he describes his symptoms, are considered to be irrelevant. The only important factors are the feelings generated at the moment he describes them.

Perhaps not surprisingly, Adler and Adlerians in general are on the other side of the argument against typology. This is because Adler was concerned almost solely with what the person *wanted* not what he was. This he called the psychology of "use" not "possession." Interestingly enough, during the 1920s and 1930s Adler was criticized for being "superficial" because he insisted that all of the individual's interpersonal conflicts were the result of immediate problems in social relationships with others. To many other schools, Adlerians today are considered old-fashioned because they consider a person's past experiences, particularly those during childhood, along with his present state of adjustment or maladjustment in his dealings with others. The reason for this puzzling phenomenon, and indeed for the disparities between the two views today, is not as difficult to understand as one might imagine. Perhaps here is where the "art" comes in.

Of course, many of these disciplines have developed into legitimate movements, and if they have broadened their scope sufficiently, are often highly successful in treating large numbers of patients. Perhaps the most impressive of these some years ago was the client-centered therapy model formulated by Carl Rogers [60]. However, Rogers, unlike many of the other practicioners in the field, was willing to subject his methods to research scrutiny. As a result, at this writing he appears to have moved in a considerable direction away from his original theory, to what might be called a more directive point of view. Others, such as William Glasser, the author of *Reality Therapy* [40], and Albert Ellis, founder of rational–emotive therapy [37], have broadened the scope of their theoretical formulations. For the most part, however, their concepts still revolve around a certain single idea, rather than a systematic attempt to explain all of a patient's personality by the how and what of the patient's present dilemma, with very little emphasis on why.

METHODS OF CURE

Two general concepts appear to have been developed with respect to so-called "cures" for patients in psychotherapy. The first is helping the patient achieve insight into the reason why he is generalizing ideas from his past with regard to a present situation. If the person is able to accept his generalization as faulty and learns not to apply what happened to him in the past to the present situation, the way is often clear for progress. Such methods are still extensively used by the more conservative of the classical Freudians, and to some extent by followers of Jung and others. The second method is accomplished by exposing the individual to a situation where he is, in a sense, pressuring him into changing his pattern of behavior in a situation where formerly his responses were faulty, though without any prior insight into why he is making the mistake. By practicing this, eventually he loses the fear of functioning positively in new situations. This is characteristic of the "homework" assignments of Albert Ellis, the "contract" system of William Glasser, and is also used by many Adlerians in family counseling, particularly with parents involving small children. It is also the method utilized primarily by behaviorists in their attempt to change a symptom that a person finds troublesome. However, in many cases, the client's behavior change is accomplished either by rewarding a new and more positive behavior, or in the case of curing symptoms such as smoking, accompanying the practice of a particular habit, by an aversive stimulant such as a mild electrical shock. In some cases, hypnosis has also been found to be helpful, simply by "convincing" an individual that the sought after behavior will give him better results and more favorable acceptance by his peers than his previous behavior.

THE DUAL APPROACH

The "homework" or "conditioning" method, as well as hypnosis, has been found to be successful often in curing symptoms that are not really fundamental to the individual's lifestyle, such as fear of flying, fear of birds, smoking, or other undesirable but not necessarily critical forms of behavior. They have, however, not been overly successful with deep-seated personality problems. The same thing can be said somewhat for the client-centered approach, which is often highly successful with those who are less severely disturbed and who have within them the resources to change their behavior merely on the basis of clarification of the problem by a therapist. But Adlerians in general believe that both insight and reeducation are necessary to bring about fundamental changes. A diagnosis of the person's lifestyle is considered essential by investigating his relationships with other members in his family. The Adlerian method of diagnosis is relatively uncomplicated in contrast to many of the other methods, and usually can be accomplished in a short time. It does not require extensive psychological testing, and with some exceptions, tends to avoid the type of typological labels such as whether the person is schizophrenic, paranoid, hysterical, depressed, or phobic. Also, under the leadership of Rudolf Dreikurs, the method of diagnosis has become simplified and structured compared to the types of earlier diagnostic workups that Adler himself used.

The factors which have been suggested as most essential by Dreikurs and his followers, but which are also the basis of diagnosis by nearly all Adlerian therapists today, consist of investigating the many environmental influences which the individual experiences during his childhood development and his interpretation of them and subsequent behavior as an adult. Diagnosing the family structure in family counseling follows some of the dynamics of adult diagnosis, but the methods utilized are a great deal different. With respect to the adult, the following questions are usually asked, with variations of course, depending on the views of the therapist.

The Nature of the Problem

The patient is asked to state why he has come to visit the therapist, how he feels and what he thinks is the nature of the problem that besets him. During this first discussion, the therapist may take no notes whatsoever and relies upon other cues of help to find the patient's situation, such as body movement, facial expressions, difficulties in communication, if any, during this interview. One question that is often used by therapists and also reveals other aspects of the person's problems is "What would life be like if you did not have this problem?" Another would be to ask the person what kind of animal he would most like to be.

Family Relationships

In examining the relationships between the individual and his siblings, the therapist not only looks for the patient's ordinal position within the family, but his own interpretation of if he felt he "fit" or not in the family constellation. In contrast to other diagnostic methods, a great deal of attention is focused on the relationship between the individual and the other children in the family, as well as that of the individual with his parents. Questions are asked, such as, "Which other sibling did you feel you were most like, and in what ways?" or, "Which other siblings were you most unlike, and in what ways?" A third step is to list a series of traits such as intelligence, school achievement, rebellion, who in the family was most gregarious, and who was favored by the mother and/or father. The individual is asked to think back to the time when he was a small child, or if he was the oldest, a young adolescent, and compare himself to other siblings then living at home as to whom he thought possessed the most or least of a particular trait. From this, the therapist very often can quickly deduce the emergence of a pattern of family induced traits.

It is interesting to note that with adults, the accuracy or deception the client manifests as to whether such traits were really possessed the most or least by other family members is not felt to be overly important by the therapist. What is most essential is to discover the client's own perception of these differences and how he feels about them.

The Relationship between the Patient and His Parents

In this process, some of the following questions are asked: What kind of a person was the patient's father in terms of personality traits? In what way does the patient feel himself most like or least like his father? The same questions are asked regarding the mother. What kind of relationship did the parents have with each other? Did they display affection toward each other? If they fought, how often, and over what subjects? An interesting question here that can be quite revealing is to ask the patient to which parent he went (if either) when he was in trouble. Also, were there other significant relatives living in the home or nearby who had a strong bearing on the individual's life? This could be an uncle, aunt, grandparent, or anyone who was living in the home or closely involved with the family.

Early Childhood Memories

To most Adlerian therapists, the most important facet of the diagnosis is obtaining the earliest childhood recollections of the patient. Adlerians consider these to be quite accurate projective representations of the lifestyle of the patient.

It is not known, but would be interesting to speculate whether Adler arrived at his conclusions about the value of early recollections on his own, or because he began to investigate them more thoroughly when he began to dispute the notion that Freud first proposed, that earliest childhood recollections were merely screen memories to hide traumatic early sexual experiences and had no diagnostic value in themselves. However achieved, it was one of the most important discoveries that Adler made. He says about memories of the individual in general,

Among all psychological expressions, some of the most revealing are the individual's memories. His memories are the reminders he carries about with him of his own limits and of the meaning of circumstances. There are no "chance" memories: out of the incalculable number of impressions which meet an individual, he chooses to remember only those which he feels, however darkly, to have a bearing on his situation. Thus, his memories represent his "story of my life": a story he repeats to himself to warn him or comfort him, to keep him concentrated on his goal, and to prepare him by means of past experiences, so that he will meet the future with an already tested style of action. [18, p. 350]

It must be pointed out, however, that though Adler considered all memory to be of value and importance in understanding an individual as well as dreams, more recent memories tended to be colored by the individual's mood at the moment he was recalling them. The very earliest memories, on the other hand, were considered to be fundamental expressions of his attitude about life and would not materially change except under the influence of an alteration in personality as the result of psychotherapy or some extraordinary revelation which would, in a few rare cases, accomplish the same purpose.

Most illuminating of all is the way an individual begins his story, the earliest memory he can recall. The first story will show his fundamental view of life, his first satisfactory crystallization of life, it offers him an opportunity to glance at what he has taken as the starting point for his development. [18, p. 351]

His statement suggests that often the very first memory recalled (which might not necessarily be the first chronologically) does reveal the individual's basic and fundamental attitude about life, while the subsequent memories appear to reflect his attempts, symbolically, to deal with life as he sees it. There have been a number of different methods by which inquiry about the memories has been made as well as interpreted. In general, what is asked is for the person to think back to a time when he was very small—what was his first recollection? A second question then asked by many Adlerian therapists is, "If you had a Polaroid camera, what did you actually see in this memory?" The purpose of this question is to determine whether this was an actual memory or one that the person might have heard from his parents and adopted as real. Then the individual is asked how he felt about the memory and how old he was at the time. It is crucial to understand that whether the memory is accurate or not is completely unimportant. What the memory reveals is a person's image of himself, how he feels about the memory, whether it was pleasant, unpleasant, or neutral also adds further insights into his attitudes about himself and others.

The age factor is of less importance unless the person is unable to recall a memory somewhere near or around the average age of an adult. The average earliest memory recollection that has been established by research has been found to be around three to three-and-one-half years old, although some people have had memories reaching back to infancy. Obviously, if a patient cannot recall anything earlier than seven or eight years of age, there may have been considerable trauma in his early life, the nature of which he does not to recall at the moment.

Additional questions, if needed, that may be relevant with respect to the interpretation of a clients's memories would be the mention of the mother or father and the attitudes toward them; whether the individual was actively involved in what was going on in the recollection or passively watching (the onlooker); recollections of punishment, danger, illness, or hurt to the individual; the first visit to school; or the birth of a younger sibling. All these are believed to have considerable importance in revealing the person's basic attitude about himself and life. If neither mother or father, nor the first school experiences are volunteered, often questions about them may furnish added insight.

THE NEED FOR BACKGROUND DATA

It is generally felt by Adlerians that recollections by themselves are not easily interpreted with nothing else being known about the individual; but in collaboration with the other data mentioned previously, these recollections provide valuable clues as to the person's underlying attitude, an attitude that may not have been revealed in his own descriptions of self and his relationships with others. There are, at times, significant exceptions to this, such as those found in a study recently completed by one of my students, Mrs. Lucy Ableser, whose thesis for her master's degree in counseling at California State University, Northridge (CSUN), was an investigation of the psychological attitudes of six children now grown up whose parents had been Holocaust survivors. I persuaded her to utilize my Adlerian work-up sheet along with her other data. The content of the work-ups of the children who were interviewed were not by themselves significantly different than those of other children of the same sex, ordinal position, and family culture, but the early recollections themselves were incredibly startling. In every case, nearly 90 percent of the individual's earliest memories were passive. In the memories, the subjects were looking, watching, were taken somewhere, but almost never indulged in any activity on their own. Things were happening to them—not necessarily negative, but the total picture was almost a surrealist's nightmare. The interpretations that emerged appeared to be the result of the fears that had been aroused in them by the behavior of their parents, *even in cases where it was revealed by one or two of the subjects that the parents had never mentioned their own personal experience during the Holocaust.* They saw themselves as onlookers in life. Any move to participate actively in relationships with others was apparently felt to be incredibly dangerous. The profiles of the individuals showed that, though they had out of necessity become more involved with others, perhaps the underlying fear and problems they had endured with their parents had in fact colored their entire lives. Several of them found it necessary to seek psychotherapy to overcome some of the feelings of withdrawal. What was so striking was that much of this would have been obscured in doing the work-ups alone, that had it not been for the patterns that were so clearly seen in the early recollections, perhaps the real insights into the perceptions of these subjects would not have been understood. Although the sample used was too small to generate a statistical analysis, the almost astonishing similarity in the passivity seen in the recollections would seem to lend considerable validity to the results of the study.

VARIATIONS IN DIAGNOSTIC METHODS

Though the type of diagnostic procedures that were developed by Adler and Dreikurs have been seen as important tools in the training of potential therapists and counselors, a considerable amount of controversy exists even among Adlerians today with regard to their use by less experienced therapists and trainees. The controversy was particularly heated in the 1940s and 1950s between the earlier Adlerians such as Lydia Sicher, Alexandra and Kurt Adler, and supporters of the approaches utilized by Dreikurs and his followers. The earlier Adlerians had consistently maintained that the type of structuring Dreikurs had proposed for diagnosis and therapy tended to oversimplify the dynamics and lead to misconceptions concerning a person's lifestyle in the process. The main reason for this objection was that although the initial principles of Adlerian theory needed to be observed, investigation into the personality was a distinctly individual process for each person. Consequently, structure could not be used. They also objected to the typology of behavior they read about in their training manuals proposed by Harold Mosak, a prominent Adlerian therapist, and others, such as the "getter," "avoider," and "martyr." It must be explained however, that in contrast to traditional descriptive diagnostic categories such as hypochondriasis, schizophrenia, or depression, the Mosak types are seen as goals of behavior within personality characteristics rather than judgments. As a matter of fact, Adler himself made sweeping generalizations in his writings about the behavior of people defined by the positions they demonstrated during sleep and the meanings behind certain specific types of dreams as well. It was also interesting to note that as they advanced in their own thinking, not only Dreikurs, but Mosak, Shulman, and Powers, and many other followers and coworkers, tended to individualize their approach to each patient somewhat the same as had Adler, Sicher, and Dreikurs. Perhaps there is not a real answer to this difference of opinion. Certainly, adult therapy is an individual affair and every person is in many ways completely unique and unlike any other person. At the same time, we are also still more alike than different in that we all have the same needs, desires, and necessities in life, but certainly interpret them differently than many others.

My own experience in attempting to understand not only the principles of Adlerian theory but to use them as a therapist and teacher was that the structure that Dreikurs proposed as a means of training not only therapist but counselors, teachers, and parents as well, was far easier to work with than the individualized approach of Lydia Sicher. The Dreikurs structure not only lends itself to work with teachers and parents, as has been mentioned, but has been effective in training many lay practitioners in such areas as family counseling and classroom disciplinary techniques. Many, even without advanced degrees, have been able to help large numbers of people, both in schools and community groups without the exhaustive training needed to become a psychotherapist. Of course, the need for rigorous training for psychotherapists is recognized by all the Adlerian training institutes and it is required as part of their curriculum.

At the San Fernando Valley Counseling Center, two followup sessions were conducted by master's degree candidates at CSUN. Both surveyed the parents who could be reached within a year to three years after counseling at different times. Of the respondents surveyed, nearly 80 percent said that significant changes had persisted. Also, several recent studies done at Brigham Young University revealed that positive changes in the behavior of children in families and in classroom settings occurred within a period of one school semester, where teachers or parents were counseled and taught the Dreikursian methods utilized in the counseling sessions reported.

It appears evident that Adlerian family counseling has an important contribution to make in the growing field of family therapy systems, and needs further investigation and research to find out the extent of this contribution and how it can be enhanced.

Chapter Ten

The Meaning and Significance of Dreams

As with many of what today are considered Adler's somewhat peripheral concepts, or those which were not regarded as crucial to the understanding of his system, his theory regarding the purpose and nature of dreams is far less known
than those of Freud, Jung, or even Jean Piaget. However, nearly all Adlerian
theorists utilize dream analysis extensively as an adjunct to psychotherapy. To
a trained Adlerian therapist, dream analysis is a valuable tool in determining the
degree of growth—or lack of it as the case may be—that the client is experiencing in psychotherapy at a time when explanation of the client's overt behavior may
be far less revealing. But as is true in diagnosis involving early recollections,
analysis of dreams is difficult without corroborating information about the
person's life. To the Adlerian, the dream reflects, to a considerable extent, the
particular circumstances the individual is undergoing at the time each dream is
recalled. However, because of dramatic new research discoveries and theories
about the nature of sleep and dreaming, it is important to place Adler's concepts
in proper context.

Many modern theorists are attempting to reassess the interpretations of Freud,
Jung, and the earlier dream therapists, but others have derived their interpretations
almost solely from the monumental discoveries concerning the process of dreaming by Aserinsky and Kleitman in 1953 [21]. Perhaps the most exhaustive and
informative early reviews of the field up to 1970 is included in *The New Psychology of Dreaming* by Richard M. Jones [51]. His review of the research up until
the time of publication is the most thorough, and his explanation concerning the
dramatic discoveries of the nature and process of dreaming which all of us undergo during our sleeping hours is most clear and concise. Unfortunately, his
analysis of dream theorists, though most exhaustive, is considerably less objective

because of his strong psychoanalytic bias. His review of Adler's contribution to the theory of dreams reveals rather strikingly many of the misunderstandings and inconsistencies present in the writings of other psychoanalysts who attempt to assess Adler's impact on psychology today. However, the conclusions that Jones draws at the end of the volume, together with his endorsement of those theorists who seem to offer the best interpretation of the meaning and purpose of dreams, seems in many ways to be much more supportive of Adler than Jones admits.

ADLER'S THEORIES ON DREAMS

Adler considered dreams, as well as other manifestations of behavior, to be direct expressions of the style of life—or, of the fictive goal. Therefore, anything contained in the content of the dream is an illustration of the basic style of life and the unity of personality. The purpose of the dream, according to Adler, is twofold: First, it is an attempt by the individual, within the context of his private logic, to find a solution to unresolved problems; and second, to provide an emotion through which the individual could approach these problems in the waking state. It must be understood that when Adler said, "Dreaming is a problem-solving process," he meant the individual may not necessarily wish to solve the problem in a realistic way and the purpose of the dream may be to warn him or frighten him away from taking constructive action on the problem. For example, Adler relates a dream of a man suffering from anxiety neurosis and agoraphobia.

This man dreamed, "I crossed the border between Austria and Hungary and they wanted to imprison me." This dream indicated the man's desire to come to a standstill, due to fear that he would be defeated if he went on. Its interpretation very well confirms the understanding of anxiety neurosis. The man wanted to limit the scope of activities in his life to "mark time," so as to gain time. He came to see me because he wanted to marry and the imminent prospect of doing so brought him to a halt. The fact that he came to consult me about the marriage clearly indicated his attitude towards it. The way he would behave in marriage was contained in the dream in which he commanded himself, "Do not cross the border." The person in the dream also reflected the dreamer's view of marriage. [18, p. 163]

ADLER'S GENERALIZED
INTERPRETATIONS OF DREAMS

Today, the trend in new books on dreams, particularly for the lay person, appears to be of the "how to" variety, with a great number of books that offer generalized interpretations of many common dreams given. What the reader is supposed to do with these views appears to vary with the writer. The meanings indicate, as does Adler, that dreams are unique to the dreamer. However, he also suggests quite a number of dream symbols that his clients appear to have in common. The list that follows offers a comparison of some of Adler's interpretations with those of a new book, *The Encyclopedia of Dreams* by Rosemary Ellen

Guiley [42]. She offers meanings for some six hundred dreams that she states come from what she calls human dream samples, which appear in art, mythology, as well as in studies by Jung, which according to her, throughout history have similar if not universal meanings. The explanations given for each symbol are drawn from historical accounts, as well as giving Jung's views on archetypes and from twenty years of dreaming recorded in the literature. She warns, however, that these are only suggested meanings to help the dreamer find the meaning of his own dreams. Here is a comparison of some of Adler's and Guiley's suggested dream symbols.

	Adler	**Guiley**
Flying	Solving of difficulties is easy: "I can do what others cannot do."	Ability to transcend. Finding reality. Resolve to escape one's earthly problems.
Falling	Fear of loss of prestige.	Out of control and lack of support.
Paralysis	Problems are insolvable.	Feels overwhelmed.
Examinations	Lack of preparation or dream is profound.	No reference.
Dead people	Dreamer has not buried his dead.	Part of grieving process. Unresolved feelings about the dead person.
Improperly clothed	Being disturbed at our own imperfection.	Unpredictability, unprepared, or afraid of exposure.
Sex	Inadequate training for sex or a retreat from sex.	Anxieties about commitment.
Homosexual activity	The result of training against the other sex rather than for cooperation.	A need to be more in touch with one's own *anima* or *animus*. No explanation of this given.
Soiling and bed wetting	Children feel they are mostly in the improper place.	Outflow of emotion, creative output, psychic waste.
Pleasant events	Contrast with existing situation, usually to provoke stronger feelings of aversion.	No reference.
Rage	Reflect the style of life.	No reference.

Adler's views on dreams probably mostly came from recollections he obtained from his patients. Guiley's findings came from dreams obtained from the public at random. However, as can be seen, the similarities of some of the detailed samples seem quite striking.

There seems such an explosion of the "how to interpret your dreams" books today, that much of the real value in the use of dream analysis now appears to have become somewhat obscured. Accordingly, it seems necessary to rely on earlier works such as Jones, which despite his anti-Adlerian bias, provides quite thorough research in the field up to the time of his publication. Guiley, however, does offer a brief explanation of some of the psychological aspects of dreams and some description of the findings of the new research in rapid eye movement (REM) sleep.

Although Adler suggested that there were common dream elements that occurred in the dreams of more than one individual, he was careful to warn that generalizations or an attempt to categorize symptoms would only partially fit some individuals and others not at all.

We cannot lay down any fixed or rigid rules of dream interpretation, we must modify each dream interpretation to fit the individual concern; and each individual is different. If we are not careful, we will only look for universal symbols and that is not enough. The only valid dream interpretation is that which can be integrated with an individual's general behavior, early memories, problems, etc. In each case, the contents of the dream should be gone over with the patient, and as many associations elicited from him as possible. [18, p. 364]

To illustrate the difficulty with which modern psychoanalytic writers have encountered in describing the relationship between the theories of Adler and Freud, it seems relevant to describe the way that Professor Jones has dealt with Adler, both in his interpretation of Adler's writing and his somewhat offhanded admission of the significance of Adler's theories on dreams. For example, Jones begins his description of Adler's contribution to the psychology of dreams by saying, "We must suspect that Adler did not remember many of his dreams, when he repeatedly spoke of dreaming in prejudiced ways" [51, p. 78]. He then cites the statement that Adler made as an example of Adler's prejudice:

The subjectively felt difficulty of the problem always acts as a test of social interest, and can be such a burden that *even the best of us will begin to dream*. We should expect therefore, that the more an individual goal agrees with reality the less we dream. We find that is so. *Very courageous people dream rarely, for they deal adequately with their situation in the daytime*. [51, p. 78, emphasis in original]

It can be seen here that Jones's emphasis on this point rests in his suggestion that Adler apparently did not remember his own dreams. From this the implication could be drawn that Adler considered himself more courageous than others. It also must be understood that Adler was basing his belief in the absence or presence of dreams on what he or his patients recalled about their dreams. No one at that time was aware of the extent to which all of us dream, and the fact that everyone fails to recall most of his dreams when he awakens, except when sleep is accidentally or purposively interrupted. Jones cites research that strongly suggests that more problem-centered individuals appear to remember fewer dreams than do others. Though Adler's generalization about dreams process can be called an error, his assumptions about the relationship between frequency of dream recollection and psychological health appears to be in agreement with the later research. This is a fact that Jones chooses to ignore.

SPECIFIC ASPECTS OF ADLER'S THEORY
ACCORDING TO JONES

Jones then goes on to state the following regarding Adler's dream theories:

Adler's writings on dream interpretation are inconsistent and often contradictory. However, since these writings may have anticipated the more orderly and thoughtful work of later theorists (notably French, Lowy, and Ulman), we are obliged to note them in passing. There are three ideas to be found in Adler's writings on dreams: 1) Dreams express the unity of personality, i.e. the dreamer's lifestyle. 2) Dreams are forward looking and problem solving experiences. 3) Dreams produce emotions which can carry over into waking life with possible adaptive consequences. Adler expressed the first idea as follows: The supreme law of both life forms, sleep and wakefulness alike, is this: the sense of worth of the self shall not be allowed to be diminished. It may be well to remark that the psychologist is not disturbed if somebody says to him, "I will not tell you any dreams." The psychologist knows that the person's imagination cannot create anything but that which his style of life commands. His made up dreams are just as good as those he genuinely remembers for imagination and fancy will also be an expression of his style of life.

Are the ways in which dreams express the unity of personality significantly different from the ways other kinds of experiences express it? This is a question Adler did not pursue, and we are unable to infer the answer from his few illustrations of dream interpretation. [51, p. 79]

It is really Jones who did not pursue. If he had read further than the quoted section in the Ansbachers's writings that he cites, it would have been difficult for him not to become aware of the numerous examples of other types of behavior such as body movements, facial expression, and handwriting, to mention a few that Adler described, *all* of which Adler considered reflections of the unity of personality and the style of life.

Jones then continues,

Adler expressed the second idea as follows: "The self draws strength from the dream fantasy to solve an imminent problem for the solution of which its social interest is inadequate. Thus, every dream-state has an exogenous factor. This, of course, means something more than and something different from Freud's 'day residue.' The significance consists in that a person is put to the test and is seeking a solution. This seeking of a solution contains the 'foreword to the goal' and the 'whiter' of individual psychology in contrast to Freud's regression and fulfillment of infantile wishes. It points to the upward tendency in evolution, and shows how each individual imagines this path for himself. It shows his opinion of his own nature and of the nature and meaning of life."

Again, Adler does not go on to say *how* he conceives dreams to seek solutions to problems, nor how they exercise their forward looking propensities, and his implicit suggestions on these points are contradictory. For example, having dismissed Freud's work out of hand, Adler's one suggestion regarding the process by which dreams seek to solve problems refers to a form of self-deception which to this writer is indistinguishable from Freud's "dream censor."

"In dreams we fool ourselves into an inadequate solution of a problem, that is, inadequate from the standpoint of the common sense, but adequate from the standpoint of our style of life. We do this by dismissing important facts and leaving only a small part of the problem which can, if everything is put to figurative metaphorical form, be solved easily. For example, a young man wants to get married but hesitates and expresses contradictory views regarding the important step he is considering. A friend may say, 'Don't be a jack-ass!' The friend thus reduces the whole complicated problem to being a jackass or not, and thus enables the young man to find an easy solution to it." [51, p. 80]

Regarding the third point, Jones cites Adler as follows:

"The purpose of the dream is achieved by the use of emotion and mood rather than reason and judgement. When our style of life comes into conflict with reality and common sense, we find it necessary, in order to preserve the style of life, to arouse feelings and emotions by means of the ideas and pictures of a dream, which we do not understand. In a dream the individual's goal of achievement remains the same as in waking life, but a dream impels him toward that goal with increased emotional power. In dreams we produce the pictures which will arouse the feelings and emotions which we need for our purposes, that is, for solving the problems confronting us at the time of the dream, in accordance with a particular style of life which is ours."

Typically, Adler immediately proceeds to imply a refutation of his own position by illustrating it with a negative case. "Thus, people frequently get up in the morning argumentative and critical, as a result of an emotion created by the night's dream. It is like a state of intoxication and not unlike what one finds in melancholia, where the patient intoxicates himself with ideas of defeat, of death, and of all being lost." [51, p. 80]

Here again, Jones misconstrues the purpose of the emotion provided by a particular dream by citing only part of Adler's quote. The portion he left out is as follows:

Let us consider, for example, the dream of a married man who was not content with his family life. He had two children, but always worried that his wife was not taking care of them and was too much interested in other things. He was always criticizing his wife about these things and tried to reform her. One night he dreamed that he had a third child who got lost and was not to be found, and that he reproached his wife because she had not taken care of the child. The result of the dream was that he had created an emotion against his wife. No child had really been lost, but he awakened in the morning criticizing and feeling antagonistic towards her. [18, p. 62]

In this example the emotion produced by the patient's dream appears to reinforce his critical attitude toward his wife quite clearly, and to Adler, obviously, the dream was a way to solve this problem in accordance with this individual's lifestyle. Again, what Jones leaves out is perhaps as important as what is quoted, and it does seem to illustrate the scope of his negative bias toward Adler's views.

PURPOSIVENESS IN DREAMS

I always remember that one of my therapists and friends, Bernard C. Gindes, used to say that if a patient consulted a Freudian therapist he would dream Freudian dreams, if he went to a Jungian therapist he would dream Jungian dreams, and if he visited an Adlerian therapist he would end up dreaming Adlerian dreams. This would suggest that we not only know which symbols to use at a given time (often some which we take from our immediate past experiences, but use in different context from the way they originally occurred), but also how and when, at will, to make them intelligible to us or even to a therapist.

LATER THEORISTS

In continuing with his chapter on dream theories, Jones quotes a number of early psychologists, commencing with Freud, Jung, Steckel, and Rank, in addition to Adler. But then he goes on to discuss the contribution of a number of the newer theorists, many of whom had the advantage of being aware of the extensive research on dreams that changed much of understanding of the nature of the dreaming process. Space is too limited here to describe all of them, and only a few will be presented that seem to bear a relationship to the views of Adler.

Samuel Lowy

His major work was *Psychological and Biological Foundation of Dream Interpretation* [52]. According to Jones, Lowy supported Jung's later formulations that the dream process, rather than being based on instinctual recall of events from the "creative consciousness," was a kind of psychic self-regulation, the purpose of which was to provide a level of what Lowy called "psycho-effective homeostasis." He said, "Just as the physical metabolism carries out the task of guaranteeing the constancy of physiological events, so have the multiform events occurring within the subconscious and unconscious spheres, the dreaming process included, to effectuate the psycho-effective hemostasis" [52, p. 86].

As did Adler, Lowy conceived the primary purpose of the dream as production and regulation of emotion. However, he did not appear to feel that the emotions thus produced had any highly significant effect on the waking activities or thinking of the dreamer unless he consciously wished it. He speaks of the "entertainment value" of the dream, according to Jones. Neither of them seem to have much faith in the possibility that the purpose of the dream was to create just the emotion that they felt in the waking state after the dream had occurred.

Thomas French

In the work of Thomas French, whose major publication with Erich Fromm was *Dream Interpretation* [39], Jones states that French's central assumption was that dreaming serves the purpose of seeking solutions to interpersonal problems. Though he infers a relationship between Adler's premise, which is much the same, Jones apparently fails to see the analogy and also the differences. French's assumptions appear to be that dreams are something of a trial and error process, largely cognitive, the purpose of which is to suggest solutions to the problem to the dreamer, which he can then use during his waking time. However, French does not appear to explain thoroughly the role of emotion in dreams, nor does he, according to Jones, explain the meanings of the symbolism with which we clothe the activities in our dreams and which we rarely can interpret without having had psychotherapy.

Montague Ullman

According to Jones, Montague Ullman was the first dream theorist to completely incorporate the Aserinsky–Kleitman discoveries in 1953, which first indicated the relationship of dreaming to the REM phase of the sleep cycle, and that all of us dream whether we remember it. Jones felt Ullman was one of the earliest theorists with the knowledge to suggest that the function of dreaming was not to preserve sleep but to maintain "an optimal state of vigilance." Jones cites Ullman as follows:

The significance of dreaming is related to the general adaptive significance of the cyclic variations in depth of sleep during the sleeping phase of the sleep-wakefulness cycle. The dream is essentially bi-directional: it may be oriented toward bringing about full arousal, or play a role in the return of sleep. [51, pp. 99–100]

This would seem to strongly support Adler's thesis that dreams are essentially purposive and of a protective nature. However, in Jones's descriptions of Ullman's theories there is no reference to Adler nor is there even any mention that Ullman's article was written as a support of Adler's views on dreams and was published in the leading Adlerian journal in the United States, *The Journal of Individual Psychology*. In the summary of the article, Ullman states as follows:

A theory of dream consciousness integrating recent physiological findings relating to sleep and dreams has been presented in summary form. A number of statements made by Adler concerning the nature of dreams were then explored within this frame of reference. Areas of agreement included the objections Adler raised to the limiting features of Freudian theory, his emphasis on the positive relationship of the dream to the lifestyle, and his emphasis on the dreamer's orientation to the future. Partial agreement occurred in connection with his discussion of the use of metaphor in dreams as a device suited to the task of stirring up feelings. A point of disagreement arose around his adherence to the self-deceptive concept of dreaming. [73, p. 25]

As can be seen, the only fundamental disagreement with Adler's views was in regard to the use of self-deception in dreaming. Ullman suggests this, as did Jones, but for a different reason. Ullman's notion that self-revelation may be more present in the dream state than self-deception seems an important insight, but it does not change the fact, which even he admits, that the *meanings* of dream content recalled are not readily understandable to the individual in his waking state. There seems little doubt that this self-revelation does occur, and perhaps frequently, when the individual dreams, but the meaning of what he remembers when he awakes is nearly always disguised. An individual who has had success-ful psychotherapy can often interpret the meaning inherent in his dream content, but for others the self-revelation Ullman speaks about can only be inferred in terms of the emotions the dreamer is left with in his waking state. However, he does not clarify this in the article to which Jones refers.

Ullman's view concerning the self-revelation purpose of dreams would seem to explain, for example, why sometimes we awaken more frequently than normal under the stress of particularly vivid or frightening dreams. However, regarding the *content* of such a dream consciously recalled by the dreamer after he awak-ens, Adler and Ullman may be talking about two different types of self-deception in the dream: The first is what is remembered on awakening; the second, that which has been revealed in the dream, but which may not be recalled by the dreamer after he is awake. To illustrate, in Adler's case of the married man who woke up with an angry feeling toward his wife, the main emotion was based on fear that his wife was not taking proper care of his children, which may or may not have been true in reality. This may to some extent reinforce Ullman's idea of self-revelation in the dream. However, when the man awakens in his anger toward his wife, he still does not know *why* he has introduced the idea of a third child to reinforce his emotional state. This is the self-deception in the dream to which Adler refers. At the moment of the dream this man sees it as a logical sequence of events, but *only in accordance with his lifestyle.* If he were aware of the true pur-pose of the dream, it would be very unlikely that on awakening he would have been able to evoke such an antagonistic attitude toward his wife. Those who have had successful therapy and are able to interpret the meaning of their dreams usu-ally find that as soon as they have perceived the true meaning of their dream, the emotion produced is dissipated almost immediately.

Perhaps a second interpretation of Ullman's self-revelation concept is that if those aspects of reality with which all of us grapple in our dreams are not in ac-cordance with our lifestyle, Adler suggests that we find it necessary to disguise them so the inconsistencies are not apparent to us in the waking state.

Since Ullman did not clarify the extent to which the self-revelation inherent in most dreams becomes apparent to the dreamer after he awakens, it would appear that he and Adler were not as much in disagreement as he had surmised.

Ullman has since gone on to become a major theorist and author in dream research.

THE LATER THEORISTS

In the latter part of his book, Jones analyzes the contributions of a large num-ber of modern theorists, including such noted psychologists as Erik Erikson, Jean Piaget, and Andreas Angyal, as well as surveying most of the more important re-search on dreams occurring up to the time of his work. However, he seems to at-tach less significance to the views these men have than to those mentioned earlier in the book. Indeed, in his final summary of the significance of the vast amount of material he studied, both theoretical and research, Jones only mentions two individuals who he thinks offered the most new promising ideas concerning the functions and purposes of dreaming. They were Frederick Snyder [67], who first reported the relationship between sleep and the amount of dreaming in both humans and the lower animal forms, and Montague Ullman.

As has been explained, Jones basically dismissed out of hand Adler's contributions to our understanding of the nature of dreams and dreaming. He cites what is, to him, the theoretical model most promising to our future understanding of why we dream at all, the vigilant hypothesis of Montague Ullman—whose thinking is probably closer to Adler's than that of any other theorist Jones analyzed.

DREAM RESEARCH SINCE 1970

Much of the studies made after those reported by Jones have tended to place more stress on the physiological nature of dreaming, as opposed to those who believed and operated on the hypothesis that dreaming was largely a psychological process. In what may be described as a more or less heretical view of the nature of dreaming, Robert McCarley, a dream researcher at the Massachusetts Mental Health Center, in an article for the *American Journal of Psychiatry* [56], suggests the following:

The nervous system does not work that way (as Freud believed), that the content of dreams is symbolic disguise for forbidden wishes. It never did and as far as we know, it never will. Dreaming is not the guardian of sleep. It is the psychological concomitant of brain activation. In other words, dreaming is largely a phenomenon of background noises of the nervous system.

We believe that the form of the dream closely parallels patterns of electrical activity that go on in different parts of the sleeping brain . . . the structure of the dream is determined not only by where the neuronal activity is going on, but also by its timing and sequences, as well as duration and intensity. [p. 64]

At this same time, McCarley does acknowledge that the motivational state of the dreamer obviously has some relationship to the nature of the dream, and for that matter, even intensity of the dream sequence during sleep. He also appears to support Ullman's thesis that most often the dream is a clear expression of the individual's motivational state and what may be revealed in the waking state. However, he does not explain clearly the meanings of symbolism in the dreams, only that it is part of the natural dream state. He also offers the rather curious notion that because

Penal [*sic*] erection and vaginal engorgement regularly occur during REM sleep, psychoanalytic theory postulates that the instinctual sexual drives furnish the energy for dreaming sleep. A more correct view, in our opinion is that the neuronal machinery underlying instinctual behavior is itself, set in motion by the activation from the pontine brain stem. Thus, for instance, a dream about sex might capitalize on this more consistently by preprogramming dreams remains to be seen [*sic*]. Nevertheless, there is growing laboratory evidence that we train ourselves to have some conscious control over our dreams, and that what happens in dreams can change our state of mind for both the next day and over time. [p. 65]

Adler alluded to a similar phenomenon, pointing out that though we may be in a state of deep sleep, we manage to maintain enough awareness to keep ourselves from falling out of bed. A mother may also sleep soundly through very loud extraneous sounds from without, but usually awakens instantly when hearing a cry from her child.

With respect to direct conscious efforts to influence the content of dreams, an anthropologist named Kilton Stewart [70] visited the Senoi people, a primitive tribe in Malaysia, in the 1950s. His reports describe how the tribe members teach their children to report their dreams and learn to control nightmares. The tribal members also attempt to train their young to take dream messages into account in their waking lives, to "adjust realities when necessary to ward off bad dreams when attacked." In the dreams, Senoi children are taught, according to Stewart, to confront and conquer the danger, and when working to change dreams, they are encouraged not to stop short of achieving a positive outcome.

In two well designed studies, Rosalind Cartwright [24] also tested Senoi methods with somewhat conflicting results. Though she found that there appeared to be a relationship between the individual's wishes before he went to sleep, it was by no means direct or clear. In her further studies, it was evident that the subject the dreamer wished to dream about appeared frequently in his dreams, but the result was not very often in the direction that he consciously wished to attain. Perhaps part of the problem might be that if what the individual wished to take place in his dream was not in accord with his goal or style of life, then obviously the content of the dream would not correspond to the wish. However, Cartwright also reported a study among a group of 271 women that appeared to confirm earlier research. Fully 80 percent said there were more times than usual that they were aware of dreaming, and they dreamed more often during times of undue stress or upset moods. When they slept more lightly, they dreamed more often. This appeared to be related to stress. She also makes a statement which seems to be nearly completely in accord with Adler's theory regarding dreams.

Dreams seem to be responsive to the level of threat we feel during the day. When we go to sleep, they take over the work of seeking solutions. Unless the problem is too big, they may manage to dispose of it within one night. If so, we will awaken in a better mood than when we went to sleep, or with our self-esteem repaired. Such a model is being tested now, to discover when and how our dreaming contributes to restoring balance to the rest of our lives. [24, p. 78]

Cartwright also cites additional research by Greenberg [41], that in general more dreaming is followed by better recall of threatening material, and that failure to dream leads to an inability to adapt to a stressful situation. This was accomplished by interrupting the individuals during periods of REM sleep. She also cites a study that she conducted with a group of psychotherapy students at the University of Illinois Counseling Service. All of them were considered poor prospects for therapy. They were divided into two groups—a control group and an experimental group. The experimental group was awakened during periods of

REM sleep and asked to report their dreams, and then discuss them. The other sixteen were not awakened. In the experimental group, progress in psychotherapy was made rather rapidly and only five of the sixteen dropped out; whereas in the control group, progress was much slower and eleven of the sixteen dropped out.

Another researcher, David Foulkes [38], working with E. Fromm, has studied the dreams of young children and affirms rather emphatically that they neither contain wish-fulfillment nor infantile symbolism as Freud depicted them, nor the archetypical collective unconscious as did Jung. They are rather simple, unemotional, and no more complicated than is the child's developing mind. Foulkes also cites Jean Piaget in suggesting that until age five or six, children do not think in terms of symbols until after they are able to organize them. Though the REM state occurs in children's dream activities as somewhat similar to adults, according to Foulkes, REM periods of ten to thirty minutes duration occur regularly, about four to six times per night, but the children are rarely able to recount what happened in these dreams the next morning. In most cases when the children were awakened during the REM state and asked to report their dreams, rarely up until age six were these dreams frightening or overwhelming. However, by age seven or eight, the dreams apparently reflect some organizational capacity as suggested by Piaget, and of course, Adler.

Foulkes's work appears to support the concept that symbols and experiences in young children, both in the waking state and while dreaming, are being organized into a unified whole as they develop. It is an interesting, though yet unexplained, finding that Foulkes also reports that nightmares among young children appear to occur primarily in non-REM sleep stages. Although they awaken with great fear, they are usually unable to describe the mental context behind their feelings. When they can, it is generally not cognitively complex, but usually described in a single word, as an expression of the emotion produced by the dream. According to Foulkes, explanations of nightmares may lie in physiology, and may be a type of unconscious panic response to the slowing of life functions such as heart rate, blood pressure, or respiration, which occur during sleep. In effect, the profound non-REM mental drama gets "out of hand."

Our evidence suggests that such dreams occur in the proportion to children's difficulties in managing their waking lives. It also suggests that anxiety dreams are not typical of any developmental stage, and that the capacity to generate unpleasant dream scenarios actually increases in step with waking cognitive development. [38, p. 88]

What appears to be so striking about Foulkes's findings and his interpretation of them is that his studies of the organization of development of symbols of children's dreams seem to follow exactly the steps by which the child organizes his experiences into a coherent, unified goal as Adler has suggested, and the age at which this organization takes place closely corresponds to Piaget's studies on the development of cognitive processes.

RELATIONSHIPS BETWEEN HUMAN
AND ANIMAL DREAMING

It can be seen that more and more modern research seems to be moving in the direction of Adler's concept as to the purpose inherent in the psychological use of dreams. Although dreams obviously appear to serve a far broader function in terms of physiological function as well as psychological development than Adler or any of the other early theorists believed or understood, what appears to be one of the more exciting developments that can be inferred from all of this is that there seems to be a direct relationship between the dreaming of lower animals and our own dreaming as was suggested by Snyder as far back as 1968. This, rather surprisingly, does not seem to have been noticed nor were connections made clearly by most of the later researchers and theorists in the field today. Part of the problem is that they may not completely understand (or believe) the holistic view that *all* our processes, whether they be dreams, physical movements, cognitive thoughts, attitudes, beliefs, or activities, are designed for a single purpose—survival. To the animal, survival means protecting itself against threats to physical well-being, so there would seem to be little doubt that the dreams of animals are designed as a form of instinctual preparation to maintain a level of vigilance that would allow them to waken quickly in response to a physical threat.

In moving this a step forward to the domain of self-consciousness, it does not seem difficult to assume a similar process occurs during human sleep, except that the major purpose of dreams—although not the only one—may largely become an effort by the individual to cope with possible psychological threats to his self-esteem. When this threat becomes severe enough, both the amount of sleep, the amount of dreaming, and the amount of dreams that are remembered increases. The individual has substituted, in effect, self-esteem for physical danger. Even in actual cases when there has been a threat to physical life, as Adler observed during his work with soldiers during World War I, the desire for cooperation and for positive relationships with others, in some of them, appeared to be as strong, if not stronger, than the need for physical survival. That those who have confined most of their research to the physiological state of dreaming appear to be less aware of this phenomenon then those who have moved into the area dealing with control and management of dreams is not surprising. An approach between the two groups seems essential, and a more thorough investigation into Adler's formulations about dreams, as sparse as they were, would seem to be very important in hastening this process.

Chapter Eleven

Adlerian Family Counseling

The practice of family counseling generally referred to as family therapy has, as many concepts in the therapeutic process, grown greatly in recent years. Since the pioneering work of Virginia Satir [61] and Samuel Lowy [52], among others some years ago, dozens of new competing theories and systems have appeared. A recent catalog, published by the Aronson Company, lists thirty-two separate books alone on various aspects of family therapy and systems analysis with, as to be expected, not a single reference whatsoever made to Adler's work in family counseling or therapy.

Adler commenced his pioneering family centers in Vienna in 1920, shortly after World War I. There had been an alarming increase in juvenile delinquency and adolescent suicides since World War I because of the poorly fed and desperate population of Vienna. The city fathers who had heard of some of Adler's work with families invited him to try to help alleviate the problem. He quickly realized that working with individual children or families in this crisis situation was not extensive enough in scope to ever approach the great needs of such a vast population, so he conceived of the idea of an open symposium to train doctors and teachers, who were the only professionals working with children at that time. In the first few training sessions, Adler himself counseled both parents and children with the professionals as the audience. This aroused some fears—particularly in those of other disciplines, notably the psychoanalysts, who openly asserted that the children might be severely intimidated by the presence of so many adults in the audience. These fears proved to be groundless. Not only were the children not frightened by the presence of adults in attendance, they even seemed to enjoy all the attention given to them by the group members. As a result of this, Adler soon decided to open the counseling sessions to anyone interested in participating, whether professional or not, and so the Vienna Adlerian Family Counseling Centers were born. At its height, there were twenty-eight such centers in Vienna alone, mostly attached to schools. The experiment also expanded to other cities and flourished until the advent of the Nazis in 1937.

Following Adler's lead, Rudolf Dreikurs came to the United States after fleeing Vienna and settling in Chicago, founding the Chicago Community Child Guidance Centers along similar lines, some of which are still in operation today.

Unfortunately, outside of the Adlerian movement itself, almost nothing is known of this technique at present. Also until recently, little has been written in the field, even by Adlerians. With the exception of a recent book edited by Oscar Christiansen [25], which describes the techniques used and also gives chapters on adolescent and marriage counseling and parent study groups, the only other writings available were a series of mimeographed monographs by Dreikurs, Ray Lowe, and others, first printed in 1959 [31]. These papers described mainly how to set up centers and operate them but contained little regarding the theory and techniques of Adlerian family counseling.

When Dreikurs came to Eugene, Oregon, in 1957 at the invitation of Dr. Ray Lowe, Professor of Counseling at the University of Oregon, he conducted the first open seminar of Adlerian family counseling in the West. Subsequent meetings, held at the Francis Willard School in Eugene, became hugely successful, drawing audiences of as many as thee hundred to four hundred people. Under Ray Lowe's influence, the centers have expanded and many continue to operate to this day.

I was fortunate enough to attend some of the early sessions in 1959 and several years later I was able to open a similar center attached to California State University at Northridge. Because of the lack of more definitive writings by others, this chapter is devoted to some of the dynamics and methods related to this type of counseling, as well as a sample interview which I conducted as part of the counseling process.

My counseling methods, though founded in Adlerian theory, are based on the tutoring I received from Dreikurs. Also, as Dreikurs had decided earlier, his focus was shifting from not just counseling parents, but in also educating teachers and school administrators in the dynamics of parent–child relationships. This also came about as a result of a breakthrough that Dreikurs achieved as a result of his Gary, Indiana, experience described in the following paragraphs. My efforts followed along the same lines.

GROWTH IN EDUCATION

As early as 1957, Dreikurs was also to undergo a fundamental change in his thinking which ultimately led him to devote a very large part of his teaching to the field of education. That year he was invited to conduct a series of classes for teachers at the school district in Gary. Until that time, he felt the principles he had developed and structured from his own experience and his dealings with Adler were best suited for parents only. But as a result of his successful Indiana program, Dreikurs soon realized that teachers, school counselors, and even school administrators could easily adapt his methods to classroom behaviors.

In 1957, largely as a result of these classes, Dreikurs published his first book on educational methods, *Psychology in the Classroom* [30]. He was then invited to teach a series of summer classes at the University of Oregon by Dr. Lowe, who had been his former student at Northwestern University. Although Dreikurs's first visits to Eugene aroused controversy, as well as acclaim, he returned in 1958, 1959, and 1960 to face an ever-growing number of enthusiastic students. In 1963, the first International Adlerian Summer School was initiated. This brought students from all over the world to Eugene. ICASSI, as it is now known, has conducted successful summer classes for educators, counselors, psychologists, and psychiatrists in Europe and Israel every year since 1963.

STRUCTURE OF ADLERIAN FAMILY COUNSELING

There have been many changes and new techniques added since the first centers were established in Chicago, but the basic Dreikursian concepts of family counseling have remained fairly consistent. The principles involved in this diagnosis and treatment, at least those in my own center, are as follows.

Diagnosis

As in all family counseling, the emphasis is not necessarily as much on diagnosing the lifestyles of the individual members of the family, but in understanding the dynamic interrelationship between members, particularly between parents and children, and among the children themselves. In the typical Adlerian family counseling session involving parents with children under the age of twelve, generally the parents are counseled separately, at least at first. Families with adolescents usually—though there are exceptions to this rule if the problem dictates—are seen all together.

When the parents are first interviewed by the counselor, the emphasis is on discovering what difficulties the parents are encountering with one or more of the children (whether disciplinary, relationship, or both). Rather than a general exploration into the personal dynamics of each child, the counselor attempts to concentrate on specific behavior problems as presented by the parent. To give a more explicit example, the following is a partial transcript of one of my own interviews with a parent (whom I call Mrs. Drake because that is not her name), her children, and an audience of about fifty people. This was held at the San Fernando Valley Family Education Center. Also sitting in with us was a student cocounselor and a master's degree candidate at San Fernando Valley State College, now CSUN.

COUNSELOR: This is Mrs. Drake. She has two children, David, who is ten and Diane who is five. Mrs. Drake, will you tell us what is going on at home?

MRS. DRAKE: David is having difficulties in school.

COUNSELOR: What kind of problems?

MRS. DRAKE: He has trouble with auditory perception and the diagnosis made by the school is what they call adult memory digital problem.

COUNSELOR: What does that mean?

MRS. DRAKE: If you ask him to repeat numbers like 7, 7, 4, 2, 9, he'll respond, "7F" and then say, "What did you say?" He's always done poorly in school. I finally got a tutor for him and took him to the college for testing to verify the school's diagnosis.

COUNSELOR: Can you tell us a little more about this?

MRS. DRAKE: He ended up at the West Valley Center for Educational Therapy. He just doesn't learn. I've had him to a lot of experts and they all tell me what they think is wrong.

COUNSELOR: Has David had a medical diagnosis?

MRS. DRAKE: Oh, yes, I took him to a pediatrician for a complete physical but nothing wrong was found. Besides the pediatrician, he was tested for reading and he's at the second-grade level. He isn't in public school anymore, but I think if he could be put on a private tutoring basis and bypass all the pressure, that he would function pretty well. Unfortunately, that isn't very realistic.

COUNSELOR: What did the test show?

MRS. DRAKE: His IQ is 116. He has lower verbal and higher performance, so that's how he averaged out to 116.

COUNSELOR: How long has he experienced this learning problem?

MRS. DRAKE: Since kindergarten. Before that he seemed average to me, but he's my first child. Once he started kindergarten, the problem began.

COUNSELOR: Do you think there could be any relationship between Diane's birth and David's experiencing learning problems?

MRS. DRAKE: Well, looking back, I would say that the problems began about that time. All of a sudden he didn't do the things most children do in the academic area of five-year-olds. He just turned himself off.

COUNSELOR: What do you think? Why did I ask this question?

GROUP MEMBER: It has to do with competition.

COUNSELOR: Yes. Mrs. Drake, has this ever been investigated by an Adlerian counselor before?

MRS. DRAKE: No.

COUNSELOR: Well, as I will illustrate to you, we have a different view from most other family counselors. Without making any conclusions, we always ask the family when the problem started and then we try and find out if it has any relationship to the behavior of another child. Whenever a new child arrives in the family, whether through birth or adoption, the entire family experiences changes. Each individual in that household has to adjust to the new situation.

MRS. DRAKE: Well, also—when I was pregnant with Diane, my older brother lived with us while going through a divorce.

COUNSELOR: How old was your brother at that time?

MRS. DRAKE: In his early thirties. He stayed about five months and then moved to Hawaii. There seemed to be a lot of competition between my brother and David.

COUNSELOR: When were you and your husband divorced?

MRS. DRAKE: Two years ago—after thirteen years of marriage. We had been married eight years when Diane was born.

COUNSELOR: In what ways, if at all, do you feel that you have become in involved in David's perceptual problems?

MRS. DRAKE: At first I was very involved because there was very little help around in finding out where to go, etc. At first I got him a tutor and that lasted about six months. David hated it. Since there wasn't any progress I took him to the college to see a Dr. Robinson at the Reading Clinic and David stayed there for one semester. Unfortunately, they weren't really into perceptual things. Since there wasn't any progress at the Reading Clinic, I took him to a Dr. Beech at the college and had him tested. Dr. Beech is the one who told me David really does have a problem. That was when David was in third grade, and he hardly knew his ABCs.

COUNSELOR: What school does he attend now, and what happens there?

MRS. DRAKE: He goes to West Valley Center for Educational Therapy. He's been there for two years.

COCOUNSELOR: What has the public school specifically said about David? Did they offer him any help?

MRS. DRAKE: No, not really. They have EH (educationally handicapped) classes, but he really does not fit that criteria. If the child has a developmental lag, he usually catches up by third grade. If he doesn't catch up, there isn't any place for him except the EH classes.

COUNSELOR: How does David like the school he's in?

MRS. DRAKE: Very much. He's comfortable there.

COCOUNSELOR: Has there been any significant change or improvement as a result of this?

MRS. DRAKE: No.

COUNSELOR: Has his reading improved at all?

MRS. DRAKE: Well, he reads a little better, but not much. When he started there he was reading at low second. What I'm most upset about is not his low level reading, but the fact that he isn't progressing.

COUNSELOR: How is he at home?

MRS. DRAKE: Well, we get along O.K. as long as there isn't a lot of pressure. But I'm a busy person and since the divorce there is a tremendous amount of work to do. I know it's hard on David, because I not only expect a lot from myself, but also from the people around me. I want them to take responsibility for themselves and for their jobs.

COUNSELOR: How often does he see his father?

MRS. DRAKE: Every other weekend.

COUNSELOR: How do they get along?

MRS. DRAKE: Fairly well, but Danny (the father) doesn't take emotional responsibility for the children. He just won't assume any responsibility.

COUNSELOR: How do David and Diane get along?

MRS. DRAKE: David's pretty protective of her, but they do fight a lot.

COUNSELOR: What happens when they fight? What do you do?

MRS. DRAKE: I try to ignore it, or sometimes I send them to their rooms.

COUNSELOR: Do you know why they fight?

MRS. DRAKE: To get my attention, I guess. I learned that by coming to these sessions and listening to other parents being counseled. I do try to get away from the fighting, but there are times, like in the morning when I have appointments and I'm trapped. I don't have enough time to be cool, or to walk away.

COUNSELOR: In other situations do you walk away?

MRS. DRAKE: When I can.

As can be seen, some of Mrs. Drake's major concerns have been presented along with possible reasons for David's behavior. Although Mrs. Drake is not sure about the basis for David's reading problem (whether psychological or medical), she is at least willing to verbalize (if not really develop a firm insight) into how it may be related to the birth of the younger child and her own divorce. However, as can be seen, the hypothesis developed so far based on inquiries regarding the children's specific behaviors, which is an essential factor for diagnosis in Adlerian Family Counseling. Now, to continue the counseling:

COUNSELOR: What you're doing is reinforcing the fighting. When you walk away, you have to do it completely. Whenever you split them up, you're responding to their provocation. That's one of the reasons they continue to fight.

MRS. DRAKE: Well, sometimes it drives me up the wall.

COUNSELOR: This behavior is what we call intermittent reinforcement, and it's just as effective as if it were continuous. That's the trouble. If you want to get out of the fights, you have to do it completely. I know how hard this is, but it has to be done. Now, if you don't mind the fighting, fine. But if it does bother you, you will have to back out of it. What other problems are bothering you?

MRS. DRAKE: Well, David doesn't do his chores very well.

COUNSELOR: That's not surprising. When it comes to chores, there are probably more relationship problems between parents and children than with nearly any other issue. Mother nags and the kids do the opposite of what she demands. However, at this point, I wouldn't worry too much about the chores.

MRS. DRAKE: But it makes me angry! I have a lot of responsibility supporting the kids and it was hard enough when we moved into the apartment. I resent the fact that I'm tired and if something needs to be done, I'm the one who does it.

COCOUNSELOR: Then why do you do it?

MRS. DRAKE: Because it has to be done—like the trash has to be taken out!

COUNSELOR: By your standards, yes. But, if there's a lot of dirty dishes around and you're too tired to clean them up, perhaps the children can get their own dinner. I think you will find, in situations like this, that if you don't push them and it doesn't become an attention-getting device, and you appeal to them by telling them that you aren't able to do everything yourself, and that you need their help, that if they don't help you, things won't get done.

MRS. DRAKE: Well, I guess so.

COUNSELOR: It has to be a two-way street. They have to understand that if the dishes don't get washed, there are no dishes to set the table with. If the trash does not get taken out, it will spill all over. If this happens, you just put it in the bedroom of whichever child has trash detail. Children can learn that cooperation is a two-way street. If you fight them on it, you can be sure they will not cooperate. Now, tell me about Diane.

MRS. DRAKE: She's outgoing, verbal, a little hyperactive in comparison to David. He gives the impression that he's placid, but he's not. When he's nervous or anxious, he gets hyper, too. Diane is the one who will just pop in, sit down, and ask your name, etc. She's much more self-assured. She's had her problems, though. About two years ago when she was attending nursery school, she wanted to be like the boys. It wasn't a joke either. She wouldn't wear dresses, she lowered her voice, and she would take off her shirt and ask everyone if they thought she was a boy. She's even put a baseball bat between her legs and said, "Look what a big penis I have." But, she's gotten over that.

COUNSELOR: Little girls often want to be boys, but she seems to be much more open about it. Do you take the children out separately—take David out without Diane?

MRS. DRAKE: Yes, but David needs to spend time with a man. He identifies with men. Even though Danny is nice to him, I'm sure he wouldn't be around if it were not for me. David's bright, he realizes that. David really needs a man that thinks David is special.

COUNSELOR: You could contact Big Brothers. They work mostly with underprivileged kids, but in a situation like this, they may be able to help. Why don't you inquire with them?

MRS. DRAKE: (NOT RESPONDING TO THE SUGGESTION) David would do anything for a man—absolutely anything. Actually, I don't have a lot of problems with the kids. Sometimes, when I'm tired, I think I do. Then I want to ship David off to his father and not handle anything. I know David does have emotional problems, but he's only ten years old, and lives with continuous stress—so who wouldn't have emotional problems?

COUNSELOR: Yes, but there seems to be no physical evidence of any actual retardation. By the way, has he ever had a neurological examination?

MRS. DRAKE: As I said, he's been to the pediatrician and there's never been any suggestion about having a neurological test. But David does suffer from minimal brain dysfunction.

COUNSELOR: How can you be sure about this unless you take him to a neurologist? Then you wold have something specific to go on.

MRS. DRAKE: (STUBBORNLY) David definitely has some brain dysfunction, because he gets his "h's" and "m's" mixed up.

COUNSELOR: I know children who are perfectly normal who do that. A pediatrician can say that he has brain dysfunction, but I wouldn't trust his judgment until David gets a thorough neurological work-up. If he does have a neurological problem, there are clinics who deal very well with this—such as the Frostig Center in Los Angeles.

MRS. DRAKE: If I take him to a neurologist, that's another $700.00. No matter what, it still won't get him to read. Even if he does have a neurological problem, he's bright enough to compensate. I can't spell and I have an IQ of 130.

COUNSELOR: Reading is important, not spelling. Forgive me for being so stubborn about this, but if David's problems are psychological, they should be dealt with differently than if they're neurological. At this point, nobody has identified the source of his problem. By the way, is David easily distracted?

MRS. DRAKE: Not particularly. He can watch television for hours, but if he gets anxious, then he's easily distracted.

COCOUNSELOR: Is he active in sports?

MRS. DRAKE: He plays handball, that's all. He's pretty well-coordinated but he won't compete in sports because he's afraid of failing. He told me he wanted to join Cub Scouts. I put him in, bought the uniform, and three months later he quit. This happens over and over again. I want you to know that there has not been much that hasn't been done for this boy, and I'm beginning to resent it.

COUNSELOR: Does he have friends?

MRS. DRAKE: He gets along fairly well with the boys in the neighborhood, but he's such a manipulator. I'm more concerned with this learning to read and to sign his name and fill out a job application when he's older.

It seems apparent that although Mrs. Drake is thoroughly frustrated in her dealings with David, she still does not want to look too closely at the psychological implications of his condition. Possibly, she may feel that if there is really not a medical problem that she herself might be responsible for David's failure to learn. There appears to be little question that she has helped to reinforce some of his behavior, but it seems evident that the handicap—whether medical or functional—is mostly being used for gaining attention from her. At the same time, Diane appears to be capturing recognition for being the "good girl," although the earlier emphasis on her wanting to be a boy might have stemmed from her seeing how much attention David was receiving.

A Typical Day in the Household

At this point, a picture of the way Mrs. Drake feels about her children has been explored, the problem with David's handicap could seem to need defusement for the moment. In most Adlerian family counseling sessions with younger children, the counselor goes through a typical work or school day with the parents. Here, other aspects of the relationship are revealed, and further problems that may be present come to light. The counseling continues:

COUNSELOR: I think there are quite a few things we can do to help David, but we do need some more information about family happenings. Why don't we go into what we call a typical day in the house, to find out more about how things run. Let's take a normal school day. Who gets up first?

MRS. DRAKE: I get up first, at 7 A.M., and call David to get up.

COUNSELOR: Does he?

MRS. DRAKE: He may sleep another five minutes, nothing more.

COUNSELOR: Does he get dressed without your nagging him?

MRS. DRAKE: Pretty well.

COUNSELOR: Do either of them need help in the morning?

MRS. DRAKE: I help Diane a little. Actually, it was a couple of weeks ago at the center when you said that if they are not ready, to pick them up and drop them off. So I told them that I would have to drop them off with shoes in hand if they weren't ready on time. I mean Diane more than David.

COUNSELOR: What happened?

MRS. DRAKE: Diane grumbled a little, but she got dressed on time. I drive Diane to school and David usually takes his bike. He does pretty well with that and it's an eight-mile ride. I do drive him if it rains, but other than that, I'm not a taxi service.

COUNSELOR: Does he like to ride his bike?

MRS. DRAKE: He prefers riding his bike than taking a bus, but he would really prefer me driving. He gets home from school about 3 P.M. Diane gets out at 3:15 and depending on my schedule, I'll pick up her up two or there times a week. When I can't pick her up, she'll stay at child care after school and I get her at 5:15. Come to think of it, I would appreciate it if David would come home from school and clean his room.

COUNSELOR: What does he do when he gets home?

MRS. DRAKE: He watches television and plays with a couple of friends.

COUNSELOR: How do things go at dinner?

MRS. DRAKE: Good. On Monday and Wednesday nights I have to go to Pierce College, so dinner is pretty short those nights. David stays with Diane while I'm in school.

COUNSELOR: How do they get along when you're not home?

MRS. DRAKE: They fight a lot, but not dangerously. David is a little jealous of Diane and he gets mad at her.

COUNSELOR: O.K. Is there anything else you want to bring up?

MRS. DRAKE: No, not really.

In a typical AFC session, the children are brought in to talk with the counselor alone at this time. This is done because the presence of the parents may inhibit the children's responses. A number of working hypotheses have been developed at this point. Mrs. Drake appears to have some insight into the children's fighting, but not much regarding other issues, and she has learned to deal with the "getting-up" problem. She has not yet learned to effectively counteract the fighting. At this juncture, it would also seem that with respect to the preliminary recommendations, that the situation has been dealt with in a somewhat mechanical, almost behavioristic manner. However, behind this, what is being attempted is to impart to Mrs. Drake two most important principles. First, that the major reason for fighting is to get her involved. Second, ignoring the fighting is the most effective way to eliminate or at least minimize the frequency. Mother has accepted the first principle, but has to be reminded that her inconsistency is defeating her ability to solve this problem. Also, Mrs. Drake's concerns about David's handicap will take considerably more time to deal with.

Although Adlerian counselors do not feel hypotheses are confirmed until the children are seen, most of the information to make a fairly accurate diagnosis is usually obtained during the first five to ten minutes of the interview. The key here is zeroing in on specific behavior a given child is manifesting, whether the behavior is negative, the response of the parents to that behavior, as well as whether it is continuing or not. It is also here in which the pioneering methods of Dreikurs provided a structure within which to analyze such actions.

THE FOUR GOALS

Adler himself saw the importance of recognition seeking as one of the major motives of human behavior, but it was Dreikurs who formulated a structure for this, by which a counselor could understand the goal that motivated the behavior of any given child (particularly that which resulted in negative interactive behavior between the child and parent). In his formulation of this, Dreikurs stated that all misbehavior that a child indulges are bids for recognition and can be divided into four general categories:

1. attention-getting
2. power
3. revenge
4. assumed disability or display of inadequacy

At this point, it is important to clarify what constitutes a misbehavior. If a child is misbehaving but is unaware that what he is doing is not what others want, attention-seeking may not be involved. A misbehavior would be a form of negative behavior that the child knows he is not supposed to do, but continues to do anyway. If the child is indulging in a misbehavior when an adult is involved, the immediate goal behind this behavior would likely be one of the four mentioned.

During the early stages of the counseling session with parents, the counselor may or may not make suggestions as to what the parent should do about the behavior, but at the same time, attempting to establish with the parents the concept that it is the need for recognition that prompts most misbehavior rather than some inherently "good" or "bad" qualities the child possesses. The counselor attempts to reveal to the parents how the position of the so-called "problem child" in his family constellation may very often have a great to do with his misbehavior, as well as the sex of each child and the differences between sibling ages.

THE RECOGNITION REFLEX

Another innovative method pioneered by Dreikurs, by which the goal behind a child's behavior can be revealed, is described as the "recognition reflex." At first the counselor attempts to set the child at ease by asking for his cooperation with the group in improving the relationship between the parents and children. Then, if the children are fighting, the counselor will usually ask them why they fight. He receives answers such as, "He did this to me," "She doesn't leave me alone," or "He pushes me." In a great majority of cases, even if the children are not severely disturbed or angry with one another, these answers are accompanied by grins, especially when the counselor asks them who starts the fights—at which time, they usually point to one another. The counselor then asks them if he could guess why he thinks they fight. A typical statement by the counselor such as, "Could it be that you were fighting to get Mother to come and pay attention to you?" or, when power is suspected, "Are you doing this to prove you can do what you want and Mother can't stop you?" If the hypothesis is one of these two, either one or both children will manifest the recognition reflex—a smile, a twinkle in the eye, a nod of the head—very often this is unmistakable, even if the child responds with a verbal no. In the case of fighting, the reflexes may be connected to different goals, but if they are achieved they are usually confirmation of the counselor's original hypothesis. This transcript indicates what happened when the counselor attempted to reveal the goals behind the children's fighting.

COUNSELOR: O.K., let's bring the children in. *(Mrs. Drake leaves the room and a student brings in the children.)*

COUNSELOR: *(To the children)* Hello, I'm Dr. Grey and you're Diane and David? How are you?

CHILDREN: Fine.

COUNSELOR: Do you know why you're here? *(The children shake their heads no.)* What did mother tell you?

DIANE: Nothing.

COUNSELOR: Do you know who these people are? *(The children shake their heads no.)* These are parents, teachers, counselors, and they are trying to learn more about how to help kids and parents get along better. Perhaps you can also help us by telling us what's going on in your home. Would you like to do this?

CHILDREN: *(Shake their heads yes.)*

COUNSELOR: You might even teach us something. Did you ever think kids could teach adults anything?

DAVID: Yeah, sure.

COUNSELOR: Good. How are things at home?

CHILDREN: Pretty good.

COUNSELOR: How do you get along with each other?

DAVID: Not very good. We fight a lot.

COUNSELOR: Who starts the fights and who wins?

DAVID: I win, cuz I beat her up, but she starts them.

COUNSELOR: Is that true, Diane? *(She shakes her head yes.)*

COUNSELOR: What does mother do when you two fight?

DAVID: Not much. She usually yells at me.

COUNSELOR: What does she say?

DAVID: I don't know—nothing much, just yells.

DIANE: Where's Mom?

COUNSELOR: She's outside. I want to talk to you without her here, because if she's here, you might not say as much. Now, why do you kids fight with each other?

DIANE: Cuz he says something I should do and I don't want to do it.

DAVID: A lot of why we fight is because I feel like her father cuz her Dad's gone. She does something wrong and Mom doesn't even do anything about it.

COUNSELOR: Do you treat Diane the way Mom treats you?

DAVID: Yeah.

COUNSELOR: Would you like me to tell you why I think you fight?

CHILDREN: Yes.

COUNSELOR: I think you fight because you want Mom to yell at you and pay attention to you.

DAVID: No. *(No recognition reflex.)*

COUNSELOR: Could it be that you fight because you want to prove that you can't be bossed by her?

DAVID: No.

COUNSELOR: No? Do you fight to get even with her? *(David shakes his head no.)* In spite of the fact that she comes and pays attention to you, you don't fight for that reason?

DAVID: She usually goes in the other room.

COUNSELOR: But, you're still winning aren't you?

DAVID: Who, me?

DIANE: Whenever she gets mad at me she says she's sorry because Daddy left and Daddy used to fight with Mommy and she fights with David the same way.

COUNSELOR: Do you think you two act like Mommy and Daddy?

CHILDREN: Yes.

COUNSELOR: So, in other words, you imitate your mom and dad.

DAVID: Yeah, and she gets mad at me all the worse.

COUNSELOR: Does she get mad at you because you don't need her?

DAVID: Yeah.

COUNSELOR: You're really mad at her. Do you want to get even with her? *(David shakes his head no.)* Well, when your mother gets mad at you, how do you feel?

DAVID: I don't know.

COUNSELOR: Do you feel angry and want to get even?

DAVID: Yeah, I guess.

COUNSELOR: Do you want to prove that you're the boss and she can't push you around? *(David smiles and shakes his head yes.) (To the audience)* That was the first reflex we got. O.K. kids, now I want to ask you a little bit about your school. David, how's it going?

DAVID: I don't know what you mean.

COUNSELOR: You go to a special school don't you? *(David shakes his head yes.)* Why is that?

DAVID: Cuz I'm behind. I can't read very good.

COUNSELOR: Why is that?

DAVID: I have this perceptual problem. I get my letters mixed up and write the wrong ones and junk like that.

COUNSELOR: Do you think Diane has the same problem? *(David shakes his head no.)* I understand that she writes words backwards too. Do you know why I think you're doing this? *(David shakes his head yes.)* I think that when Diane was born you started having this trouble.

DAVID: Did Mom say that?

COUNSELOR: No, this is my idea—that all this started because you were no longer the center of attention after Diane was born and you decided you didn't want to do anything and were unhappy about the whole thing. Then your dad left and it made things worse, so now you just let others do things for you because you're "poor David." What do you think about that?

DAVID: *(Smiles slightly.)*

COUNSELOR: Well, it's a possibility. I think that when you want to learn you will. You can learn reading or anything else you want.

DAVID: I want to. My teacher even says I try sometimes.

COUNSELOR: Well, usually if you wait this long to learn you find it takes longer. You have to start earlier, but I think you can do anything you want, and your problem is not so much that you can't learn, but the way you feel about things. What do you think of that?

DAVID: I'm not sure I can. It's hard.

COUNSELOR: I didn't say it was easy, but I said you can do it.

DAVID: I don't know. I try my hardest, I do my school work.

COUNSELOR: Do you think that if you really started working hard every day that Mother would pay as much attention to you?

DAVID: I don't know.

COUNSELOR: Think about that. You have to decide this for yourself. I believe you can do anything you want. Very often kids will decide that working hard isn't worth it. Then Mom gets all excited and sends you to a special school and you get a lot of attention. It's easier to stay there and not work that hard, but later on, if you don't learn to read, you can't get a driver's license and you have all sorts of problems.

DAVID: I'll learn to read that good!!

COUNSELOR: So, you'll learn to read. Well, that's fine. I've enjoyed talking to you. I want to ask Diane a couple of questions. Diane, Mom says that whenever something happens, you run in and tell her that you're afraid of David. How do you get along with your brother when Mom's not around? Does he hit you?

DIANE: Well, sometimes I'm scared—when he gets mad. He doesn't hit me, but he acts like Daddy did.

COUNSELOR: Is this when Mommy is not there?

DIANE: Yeah, sometimes I sass him and when we fight, he gets mad.

COUNSELOR: Just like your father? How about getting up in the morning? Mommy says you used to dawdle and not put clothes on in time to leave. What happened to change that?

DIANE: Well, I was tired. Last night I really got tired because I watched TV so late, but I still got dressed on time today.

COUNSELOR: That's very good. Well, I enjoyed talking with both of you and really appreciate your coming. Thank you, and we will see you again. *(The children leave and Dr. Grey asks the group what they thought.)*

GROUP MEMBER: How much do you think David got from what you said to him?

COUNSELOR: It's not really important. I told him what he did on purpose because I want him to look at the idea that there might not be anything really wrong with him. He's got the description of his perceptual problems down pat, but I don't believe he really knows what that means. What I was doing was trying to reveal the goal to the child. I didn't get much response on the fighting with each other because I think they are imitating their parents. They really fight for their own benefit because what Mrs. Drake tries to do doesn't seem to have much bearing on it. However, I have a feeling that much of this behavior is what we call a "power struggle" between David and his mother. Now, would someone please bring Mrs. Drake back into the room. *(She returns.)*

COUNSELOR: It was an interesting session, particularly with David.

MRS. DRAKE: What did he say?

COUNSELOR: Well, he certainly knows that he has a perceptual problem and even that he gets his letters mixed up. He's blaming all of his reading problems on the fact that he gets his letters mixed up.

MRS. DRAKE: Isn't that what it is?

COUNSELOR: As I have mentioned, we cannot be really sure what the actual basis of the problem is, but he certainly uses it to get recognition from you. It serves his purpose at this moment because he knows how to bother you. I'm not saying there could be no physiological component in his problem, but it is important for you to see what he does with it. For instance when I told him that he could learn anything he wanted, he responded, "It's not easy." When I told him that I hadn't said it was easy but that he'd have to learn to read to get a driver's license, he told me quite emphatically that he would learn to read well enough for that. This suggests to me that he will learn when he really wants to.

MRS. DRAKE: Since I've been coming here, I've been trying to take the pressure off, but I, too, get anxious.

COUNSELOR: Part of the problem has to do with the amount of pressure you have. You're busy with so many things. David's being deliberately opposite because he knows it bothers you. You're right in keeping the pressure off him. Just let him decide what he wants to do. It's the only way you can handle something like this. I'm going to go out on a limb and say that I think he's physically all right, but a neurological work-up is the only means of determining this positively. I don't see this boy as severely discouraged. He's got a good thing going, and as long as he's got a good thing going, he's going to continue. I believe that when he gets ready to get himself out of it, he will.

MRS. DRAKE: I hope you're right and after listening to you, I can see that David is aware of what's going on.

COUNSELOR: Certainly he is. Very much so. Since you have begun to take the academic pressure off of him, you should now begin to take some more pressure off of him at home, too. As far as the chores are concerned, you need to let up on both children, with the one proviso that if they don't do what they're supposed to, you won't do what you're supposed to. I think you have a good enough relationship with them so that you can successfully do this. You also need to think about the fact that you're angry with David and he's angry with you. Most of his anger is due to the fact that you're gone so much and he has no father.

MRS. DRAKE: Well, yes I do know that I'm angry and I feel guilty about it.

COUNSELOR: Well, it may take more than that. You have to consciously think of when you get yourself into these jams with him to walk away from them and at other times to provide more encouragement and support. I realize that you're very busy, but you do love this boy and you are responsible for giving him the encouragement he needs. When you find yourself getting angry, walk away instead of nagging and badgering.

MRS. DRAKE: Do you think David and Diane's relationship is O.K. with each other?

COUNSELOR: Fairly good, except that it's somewhat like a father–child relationship rather than a brother and sister. Diane's a little frightened of David sometimes because he acts like a father and treats her like a child. But I think they are pretty close, even though he assumes the father role.

GROUP MEMBER: They have each other.

MRS. DRAKE: Yes, I see that. I tell him that he doesn't have to take responsibility for Diane, but then I turn around and give it to him. I'm trying to give the responsibility to the babysitter.

COUNSELOR: Just let David handle it in his own way. I think you should follow through with Big Brothers. If that don't work out, find a friend or relative who could act as a father figure to David. Now, about Diane. She seems quite self-assured. In fact, I didn't see any real discouragement in either one of them. David could very easily act discouraged and feel sorry for himself, but he doesn't. As I said before, my feeling is that he's got a good thing going and he's going to continue as long as it works.

MRS. DRAKE: I always tell him that being different doesn't mean being bad.

COUNSELOR: He's not different. He has not caught up yet academically. He's a little lazy and he's going to begin feeling pressure as he gets older. It will take him a while to catch up, but he's not in serious trouble even though his academics are deficient.

MRS. DRAKE: I know that I need to spend more time with the kids, but I'm so busy and feel so much pressure to make a decent life for all of us.

COUNSELOR: With children, it isn't the length of time you spend with them, it's the quality. Somehow this is not coming through. I also think a family council would benefit all of you.

MRS. DRAKE: I've heard you discuss it and we have tried it.

COUNSELOR: How did it go?

MRS. DRAKE: I didn't like it too well. I gave them a choice of what they wanted to do and then we did it.

COUNSELOR: It's more complex than that. You don't just let them make decisions. A family council is where all of you get together at a convenient time regularly and talk about the problems that relate to the household, particularly chores, and possibly make plans to take family outings together. I suggest focusing on a family outing for the first meeting because this is something that children usually want to do, so they will want to participate in the meeting. After the first meeting, the chair rotates, with someone different taking the notes each time. In regard to an outing, instead of you deciding where to go, all of you decide among yourselves. You all vote on it, and of course, it has to be something within your financial means. If the kids suggest something out of your means, you just tell them that you cannot afford it. What's most important about a family council is the regularity of the meetings—at least once a week. The kids have the right to air their gripes, etc. When it comes to chores, have a sign-up sheet where all of the chores that need to be done are listed. Then have a separate list of chores that aren't as necessary, but still need to be done. You then all make choices as to what chores you will each do for one week, and let the kids make the first choices. After you've done this, there will be some chores left and you draw straws for who is responsible for them for one week. At the next council meeting, you begin the process all over again. By doing this the children will have the opportunity to see that this is a family group, and that you all have a share. The family council has often been very successful in bringing about a group feeling of pulling together. Do you have any questions about this? Would you like to bring up anything else?

MRS. DRAKE: Only that I wish David had more drive and ambition.

COUNSELOR: We have covered this pretty well, but I would like to emphasize that because you have so much drive, it's very easy in a family like yours. I would like you to give this some thought. You indicated earlier that your husband, Danny, also showed very little drive.

MRS. DRAKE: Yes, it was impossible to deal with him. He was polite and all that, but he would come home, flop on the couch, and watch TV all night. That's not O.K. with me. And it's my drive and ambition that gets all the work done.

COUNSELOR: You can farm out some of those chores by using the family council. If they don't get done—they don't get done. You can learn to relax and not be so uptight. Give the council a try, and remember, the secret lies in getting things to where they are a family group deciding on what to do rather than your arbitrarily ordering them. If you end up doing the chores, children quickly learn to out-wait you. Being a perfectionist is not bringing the results you want.

MRS. DRAKE: I keep thinking that if David is O.K. with me that he will be O.K. with himself.

COUNSELOR: I think just the opposite. When David is O.K. with himself, he will be O.K. with you. Don't worry about how he is with you. I think we have made a good beginning here. How do you feel about this session?

MRS. DRAKE: Pretty good. It has been helpful, but it sure seems as though I've got a lot to work on.

COUNSELOR: Just concentrate on the one particular problem and solve that before moving on to others. I would suggest you begin by backing down from all the pushing of David that you do, and to utilize the family council. That is going to be enough for you to do at this time. Keep coming to the sessions here and we'll meet again in two or three weeks.

After the family leaves there is a general discussion among the group. Members are given the opportunity to ask questions and make comments on the progress of counseling. Although the followup sessions with Mrs. Drake were not taped, she did report some positive changes in her household. Even though she contradicted herself in the first session, she did have some awareness and was able to begin moving in a positive direction. She never took David for a neurological work-up, but the improvement in his schoolwork suggested that it may not have been necessary.

COUNSELOR TRAINING

Although training methods vary among Adlerian family counseling centers, the presence of the group affords many excellent means of counselor training. In addition to utilizing a cocounselor at most of the sessions at the San Fernando Valley Center, each student in the audience is asked to make notes of each session and present them in a log at the end of the semester. Also, at each session an individual student is requested to complete a record format of the counseling session which is then placed in the family file.

The attached examples are from two separate counseling sessions for the same family, and recorded by the same student. As the transcript just concluded in this chapter was of an initial session, it was felt to be appropriate to show record formats of two continuous sessions; in this case, the fourth and fifth times the family had been to the center, although not on a continuous basis.

The format also gives a playground observation report on the children of the family who are being seen. This has been found to be an extremely valuable addition to the understanding of the nature of the family problems and to reveal possible changes in playground behavior from one counseling session to another. The format also helps the trainee focus on the essential dynamics of the family relationships, behavior goal of the children, and recommendations to the parents as to how to accomplish behavior changes by the children.

RECORD FORMAT

NAME OF FAMILY: B. (stepfather);   L. (mother);   fourth session

COUNSELOR: Dr. Grey

COCOUNSELOR:

FAMILY: List all the children in the family with their ages in descending order, regardless of whether those children are all present. Put a (*) next to the child about whom the parent is most concerned.

*Robin, age 8, boy   Angela, age 5, girl

Interview with Parents:

Make clear whether one or both parents were present at the interview. Delete counselor's explanation while editing and place under summary.

Both mother and stepfather present.

Nature of the Problem:

Mother and stepfather had been to counseling previously. Robin had not been getting along at school. Teachers reported he was rude, fought, did not work, and was always dirty. They felt that things improved when they followed the counselor's suggestions, but recently things had deteriorated, and they had returned to counseling. Robin had taken money from school and from home. He was not doing the one chore that he had elected to do at a family meeting. He was involving his grandmother in situations that were upsetting at home.

Parents' Basic Mistakes:

Robin's mother is very involved at this time with school and working. She does not spend much time with Robin. Robin sees his real father on weekends only. Robin's stepfather does not spend much time with Robin. Mother says that the stepfather will involve Robin in power struggles and has teased him in the past. Parents' attempts at logical consequences have backfired.

Goals of Children:

Robin's goal appears to be revenge. He is angry with his parents. He is using every situation he can to get back at his parents. He is telling the parents that he feels they are against him. He does not feel loved. Robin is also playing off his grandmother against his parents for attention and as another means of gaining attention.

Interview with the Children:

Include here only the names of these children present at this interview. Record actions as well as words. Leave all counselor's explanations and recommendations intact, in the context in which they were offered. Do not interpret.

Robin is a small-sized boy. He appears dirty and disheveled. He is extremely noncommunicative. He answered "fine," when asked how things were at home. He answered no when asked if his stepfather still teased him. He maintained that he did not do his chore of taking out the trash because, "I only have one chore, but he asks me to do other things." When asked about his clothes, he said he did not like to wash them. He would not respond to questions involving why he thought he did things. He said yes when asked if he thought that Mommy worked too much. He became belligerent when it was suggested that he found the money at home and said, "I found it at school." When asked what could the stepfather and mother could do to make things better at home, he responded, "Be around more." What could he do? Do his chores.

Playground Report:

Include a brief summary of the oral report given by the Playground Director. Robin was reported as being aggressive the entire time he was on the playground.

He built a house with blocks, tearing down the houses of others when he wanted their blocks. He knocked down a little girl who cried. He showed no concern for any of the other children, said he did not care if they got hurt. He told another little child to "go away." He said he did not like to come to counseling. The director observed that he seemed very nervous. He was independent. He built complex structures with the blocks. He did not share or cooperate. He was always on the move.

Summary:

Include all counselor's explanations and interpretations made to parents.

Counselor: Robin is a manipulator. He is playing all parties against the other. Robin took the money to get even with his parents. He is angry with them. He feels that his parents are against him. Parents used some of the methods in good faith, but because Robin is motivated by revenge, the methods did not work. Logical consequences must be done in a calm and friendly manner. If there is any anger or punitiveness attached, it destroys it. The stepfather may be guilty of this. Robin feels pushed out by his parents's life because they do not spend sufficient time with him to let him know he is wanted and a member of the family.

General Observations:

Includes all the counselor's general recommendations made to the parents.

Spend more time exclusively with Robin now. This was the major recommendation, especially to the mother. Take off all pressures until Robin feels accepted and wanted, then you can go back to using the techniques again. Mother should organize her life so that Robin has a higher priority and that he is aware of it. Encourage him as much as possible. Don't worry.

Specific Recommendations for Each Child:

Include the specific areas the counselor recommends the parents should concentrate on for each child.

Return to washing Robin's clothes. Try to get him to put clothes in hamper. Spend time alone with Robin. This should be more the responsibility of the mother, and the stepfather should also do things alone with Robin.

RECORDER: D. H.

RECORD FORMAT

NAME OF FAMILY: B. (stepfather);   L. (mother);   fifth session
COUNSELOR: Dr. Grey
COCOUNSELOR:
FAMILY: *Robin, age 8, (male)   Angela, age 5, (female)

Interview with Parents:

Stepfather and mother present.

Nature of the Problem:

The parents were returning after three weeks. They reported that they had moved into a large house which had alleviated some of the problems. Both seemed to feel that things were going better, and that Robin was doing better. However, they added that they had not been able to put some things into practice due to the move. Some additional problems that Mother noted were: Robin wearing socks outside without shoes, putting too much milk on his cereal, bullying a small neighbor, and fighting with sister. Grandmother still a problem. Robin still wetting bed. Angela uses baby-talk.

Parents' Basic Mistakes:

Since mother had spent more time with Robin than had stepfather, it seemed Mother was finding more fault with the boy. She is still responding to situations that Robin sets up for the purpose of getting her attention. She continues to want to feel that her efforts will always be thwarted by the grandmother.

Goals of the Children:

Angela competes with Robin for attention. Robin, as stated in an earlier write-up, seeks attention, power, and possibly revenge. He is angry with his parents for not making him feel loved and having a place in the family. Robin becomes the first child when Angela is there. At other times, he is the only child. He uses grandmother to get back at his parents.

Interview with the Children:

Robin and Angela came in and sat down. Robin was smiling. He said things had been going fine. He talked about his new house. When asked whether he and Angela ever fought, he said "Sometimes," and Angela said "No." When the counselor suggested that they fought to get the parents to pay attention to them, Robin would not admit it, but Angela did. Robin seemed confused on the washing of his clothes issue, but he smiled when the counselor said his clothes would be washed if he put them in the hamper. Shook hands with the counselor and left.

Playground Report:

The Playground Director observed a considerable improvement in Robin's behavior on the playground. Said he was not domineering to other children as much. Angela followed Robin around. Robin was constantly seeking the adult's attention. He was in constant motion.

Summary:

Dr. Grey indicated to the mother and stepfather that they still have some progress to make with Robin. They won't know how successful they are until Robin returns to school. Robin misbehaves at school for their benefit. When they improve the situation at home, things at school will change. It is necessary that the mother and stepfather work with Robin on their own. Let the grandmother do her own thing.

General Recommendations:

Continue the past suggestions. Try to ignore the negative behavior and encourage the positive. Spend more time with Robin, especially Mother. Continue to wash his clothes. Ignore fighting of Robin and Angela. Walk away.

Specific Recommendations for Each Child:

ROBIN: Put hamper in his room. Get a waterproof pad for the bed and don't pressure him on bed wetting.

ANGELA: Ignore her baby-talk. She does this for attention.

RECORDER: D. H.

As the transcript and record formats reveal, Adlerian family counseling involves a good deal of advice-giving, which is almost completely contrary to any other counseling therapeutic methodology in practice today. One might ask the question, Why does it work when most advice given to adults in a therapy setting is usually ignored? Dreikurs's response to this question was that most parents who were willing to be counseled at all would change their behavior to help their children improve, even if they resisted it for their own benefit. He also indicated that, in his experience, he had seen even severely disturbed parents make considerable progress in improving relationships with their children through the use of Adlerian family counseling.

At the San Fernando Valley Counseling Center, two followup sessions were conducted by master's degree candidates at CSUN. Both surveyed the parents who could be reached within a year to three years after counseling. Of the respondents surveyed, nearly 80 percent said that significant changes had persisted. Also, several recent studies done at Brigham Young University revealed that positive changes in the behavior of children in families and in classroom settings occurred within the period of one school semester, where teachers or parents were counseled and taught the Dreikursian methods utilized in the counseling sessions reported.

It appears evident that Adlerian family counseling has an important contribution to make in the growing field of family therapy systems and needs further investigation and research to find out the extent of this contribution and how it can be enhanced.

Chapter Twelve

Alfred Adler and Rudolf Dreikurs

As was mentioned in the beginning of this book, Adler once stated that within this century his ideas would be universally utilized by nearly everyone in the mental health field, but few would recognize them as his. Though this prediction appears to have come true, there is still little growth toward a more direct understanding of Individual Psychology by those in psychology and education throughout the world. What progress has been made may be due more to the energy and dynamism as well as the reinterpretation and innovativeness of Rudolf Dreikurs, than perhaps anyone else among Adler's students and co-workers.

This is not to diminish in any way the contributions of the Ansbachers, Lydia Sicher, and Paul Brodsky in Los Angeles, Erwin Wexberg, Sophie DeVries, and Lucy Ackernecht in the San Francisco area, and Adler's children, Alexandra and Kurt, who are among the many who have established clinics and wrote voluminously throughout the world to disseminate Adlerian ideas in what was, in those early years, an unsupportive and often hostile environment.

However, Rudolf Dreikurs brought two very notable innovations into Adlerian psychology, which had not been recognized thoroughly until the last twenty years, when the impact of his work has been felt. The first was his restructuring of Adlerian concepts to make them more easily understood by those who utilized them, whether they be psychologists, psychiatrists, teachers, lay counselors, or even parents working in study groups. Into this structure, he contributed many of his own ideas. The second was his insistence that Adlerian ideas could only be spread through a genuine mass movement, not limited to those holding advanced degrees or having been exclusively trained in Adlerian principles, but simply by anyone willing to join the group. A third factor—although this was one which Adler himself had recognized as important much earlier, though he had not been as able as Dreikurs to capitalize on it effectively—was that schools could become the most important instrument for the dissemination of Adlerian concepts and methods.

ADLER AND DREIKURS

As was mentioned earlier, it was in the Oregon schools, under the leadership of Ray Lowe from the University of Oregon, and Maurice Bullard of the Corvallis School District, that Dreikurs first launched the Adlerian movement as a major basis of school and community activity. Dreikurs was courageous enough, perhaps to the detriment of his own notability, not to assert that his contributions were entirely his own, as did a number of other well-known figures in the mental health field. He steadfastly affirmed that the new methods he proposed were derived almost entirely from Adler's original theory. But the innovations and creativity that Dreikurs brought with him in his interpretation and application of Adlerian theory displayed a genius that was much his own and one very different from that of Adler. At this same time, even though they both had highly divergent lifestyles, their careers and even their physical appearances in later years showed astonishing similarities. In the years of their highest intellectual powers, both men were short, rotund, with round jowly faces, and rather sparse hair. They both wore glasses and sported small, neatly trimmed moustaches. Both of them, until the day of their final illnesses, possessed amazing energy. They both grew up in prewar Vienna and were actively involved in the intellectual turmoil and discovery that laid the foundations for psychotherapy as we know it today. Though Dreikurs was a first child and Adler a second, both were rebels, not so much against parental authority, but against the authority of the dictatorial leaders of their day. Each of them worked, for a time, with political movements that were striving to overturn this authority. Both were compassionate and caring men who believed in the innate goodness of all mankind and were singularly devoid of the sexual and racial prejudices that were so prevalent in their day. Both suffered individual personal tragedies as a result of the Holocaust and the Stalinist dictatorship, which destroyed relatives and friends alike, and wiped out their movement in Vienna and the rest of Europe. Both were deeply troubled about the turbulent, almost psychotic state of human relationships, and spent the major part of their adult lives tirelessly attempting to show their fellow human beings that the resources to change themselves and make a better world were present, if people would only listen and understand.

Despite the ominous warnings of the consequences of what was happening immediately around them, both remained unflaggingly determined to reach out to as many people as they could during their lives. Somehow they believed the resources they developed could one day be used to create a world where war, poverty, violence, and the most grievous mistakes in interpersonal relationships would be mitigated, if not entirely avoided. Both saw the United States as the social laboratory where ultimately the new and terribly painful concepts of equality and freedom would be put to the test. Each of them lived to see their ideas take root in a modest way in American soil. Both men were uniquely different, but in many ways that contributed to their success, and at the same time created handicaps for themselves and their followers.

Though I never met Adler, much of what I did learn about him came from Lydia Sicher, who perhaps knew him more intimately than anyone in the movement. Though Adler and Dreikurs were both brilliant therapists, Adler was the warmer of the two and somewhat more intuitive, but unfortunately he was not always able to explain the meaning of how his intuition was related to his theory. Thus, it was left up to his followers and those who observed his therapy sessions and listened to his lectures to impart understanding to others. As a result, though Adler was a brilliant lecturer, he was apparently not as notable as a teacher. Dreikurs, on the other hand, was always careful to analyze his intuitions and as a result was able to explain them when asked.

DREIKURS AS A TEACHER

I once asked Dreikurs why it was possible that anyone could stop him at any point in one of his counseling sessions or lectures when he revealed one of his insights and ask him why, and he was nearly always able to come up with the answer. His reply to me was that he had become so frustrated when Adler often could not explain where he derived his insights, that he was determined to analyze his own thinking in a way that could be readily comprehended by anyone who was willing to listen to his lectures and seminars. As a result, Dreikurs was by far the more masterful teacher of the two. It was this analysis of his own insights that helped him formulate a structure of concepts which helped him to make the whole Adlerian theory more intelligible than it had previously been known. On the other hand, Adler apparently was a somewhat more gregarious person than Dreikurs and enjoyed a wide circle of close friends during his lifetime—a characteristic that appears to be found much more often in a second child than in a first.

DREIKURS THE BATTLER

On the other hand, by his very pugnacity and authoritarianism, Dreikurs often offended many who were closest to him. In his bitter struggles during the early years of his career to just survive in a hostile professional environment, this quality was to prove a virtue. But in some cases during his later years, it became a handicap. He often antagonized many who might have become his supporters and friends in his lectures and demonstrations. He rarely was able to accept opposition or criticism. His domineering style and sarcasm often made it impossible for anyone to counter his arguments—even if his concepts were mistaken. At the same time, those who stayed and were willing to endure these mannerisms were able to discover the astonishing revelations in many of his insights and his ability to describe the essentials of each in detail. Ultimately, many of them became devoted supporters and followers. Though both men shared the ability to lead and inspire those with whom they came in contact, it was Dreikurs who had the clearest idea of in what specific direction this leadership should move. Wherever he went, he always sought out those who would be willing to carry on the principles he espoused when he was gone. He was nearly always prepared with a planned strategy on how to carry this out.

ADLER AND DREIKURS AS WRITERS

Neither Adler nor Dreikurs possessed a mastery of writing like Freud, but Dreikurs was the more organized writer of the two. Perhaps Adler's most brilliant piece of literary craftsmanship was *The Neurotic Constitution* [2], first written in 1912, when he was a member of Freud's circle. In his book, his accounts of the development of the fictive goal, the assumption of fictions and the style of life, as well as the concept of the relationship between men and women were at the time unknown concepts, but carefully and in some instances, most effectively presented. Unfortunately, because he had not reached the final stage in the evolution of this system, much of the value of this book was obscured because of his assumption that, as was mentioned in Chapter One, the will to power was the ultimate goal behind personality.

Consequently, after some brief interest in his books among professionals in the 1920s and 1930s, Adler's ideas were virtually forgotten until the publication of *The Individual Psychology of Alfred Adler* in 1956 [18].

Dreikurs's writings were, however, a good deal more systematic and less general than Adler's. His early books, *The Challenge of Marriage* [28] and *The Challenge of Parenthood* [29] were designed for the lay public and were more practical and down to earth than Adler's writings had been. They enjoyed a good deal more success in their early releases. Both books have been revised and reprinted and are available in print today. *Psychology in the Classroom* [30], published by Harpers in 1957, was the first of its kind written by an Adlerian, and offered many concrete and specific ways by which teachers in this country could improve relationships with children in their classrooms. Adler had also written a book entitled *The Education of Children* [11], but it followed to a great extent the format of books such as *What Life Should Mean to You* [14] and as such, was more of a book on theory than on methods in the classroom. Oscar Spiel and Ferdinand Biernbaum had also collaborated on a book entitled *Disciplining without Punishment* [69], which offered many insights and techniques they had learned while conducting their experimental Adlerian school in Vienna in the early 1920s, but the English translation of this book was not published until after *Psychology in the Classroom* [30]. The original version of the latter title has remained almost continuously in print without revision to this day.

Also, whereas Adler rarely, if ever, wrote with collaborators, Dreikurs was quick to realize the value of utilizing the talents of many of his associates in clarifying and defining many of his and Adler's concepts that had not been adequately documented before. The result of this was the outstandingly successful book *Children the Challenge* [32], written in collaboration with Vicki Stoltz. I was fortunate to be associated with him on two books: *Logical Consequences: A New Approach to Discipline* [33] and *Parents' Guide to Child Discipline* [35]. Both are still in print today. Other important collaborations were *Maintaining Sanity in the Classroom* with Ray Corsini, Floy Pepper, and Bernice Grunwald [36]; and a manual on family counseling done in collaboration with Ray Lowe and Bina Rosenberg [31].

FURTHER APPLICATIONS OF DREIKURS'S WORK

There were a great many other major contributions Dreikurs made that not only aided materially in understanding Adler's philosophy, but at the same time added his own unique skills and understandings to his knowledge. The recent brilliant biography of Dreikurs entitled *The Courage to Be Imperfect: The Life and Work of Rudolf Dreikurs* by Janet Turner and William Pew [72] gives a much more detailed description of Dreikurs's contributions than can be given here, and therefore only the most important are described.

Family Counseling

In his format of family counseling, Dreikurs's method of application was essentially similar to that of Adler—a counselor–therapist interviewing the clients or family in front of a group who would not participate in the counseling process as equals, though they might be allowed to ask questions. Whether this might be considered undemocratic does not essentially violate the premise that both Adler and Dreikurs themselves discovered too many suggestions from the group during the counseling sessions, in that it might tend to confuse the clients. Interestingly enough, the methods of Adlerian family counseling, as practiced by Adler and Dreikurs and present-day Adlerians in the field are still quite controversial, but for different reasons. In the beginning, both Adler and Dreikurs were attacked savagely by the Freudians who considered it humiliating and damaging to have children spoken to in front of a group. Such opposition to this technique has long since disappeared. Criticisms concerning the Dreikursian technique now center mainly around the fact that the counselor is seen as giving "advice" or "telling" parents what to do. It is probably true that this may be the only established form of counseling in psychotherapy where such methods are consistently used.

However, the continuing progress of the Chicago Child Guidance centers—as well as those in such states as Oregon, Arizona, Minnesota, and Delaware, to mention a few—is represented by the followup surveys given to parents attending or having been counseled at these centers, which reveal that the relationships between children and adolescents can improve significantly, and that these changes persist over a period of years.

As might be understood, the influence and degree of control parents can exercise over children up to age twelve is considerably greater than when attempting to discipline older children. At the onset of puberty, adolescents become more critical of parents, less amenable to either their suggestions or their control, and gravitate much more toward peer influences. However, centers that involve both teenagers and parents and that allow a much greater degree of group participation have been found to have a great deal more success than in those centers that are more counselor oriented. Though Adlerian principles are still the underlying basis, because of the suggestions offered by counselors or group members, these sessions have a greater similarity to encounter groups, rather than to those described in Chapter Eleven where the children are younger.

In dealing with preadolescent children, the procedures utilized, though essentially fairly simple, are most profound, and have not been well understood until Dreikurs did his pioneering work on family counseling following the Adlerian method. Parents will generally follow through on advice and suggestions for improving the relationship between themselves and their children more readily than they would suggestions about changing their own behavior or their relationships with the other adults around them. Dreikurs mentioned this more than once in his demonstrations and workshops. He also suggested that even schizophrenic parents, in some instances, can make things better between themselves and their children, as long as they were in contact with reality at all and were able to follow through with the counselor's recommendations.

Group Psychotherapy

Interestingly enough, the term "group psychotherapy," was coined by Jacob Moreno, now known for his pioneering work in psychodrama and sociometry. However, most of Moreno's work with groups consisted of using them as a formal audience where he could practice the demonstrations of his techniques of psychodrama, for which he ultimately was to become famous. Although the use of group members to help one another within the process of group psychotherapy was not original with Dreikurs, he was one of the earliest psychotherapists to move the setting out of the clinic or hospital and into private practice, as well as the first president of the American Group Psychotherapy Association. Dreikurs also began to recognize even before he came to America that in a democratic atmosphere, very often individuals relating to one another can provide more therapeutic insight to each other than can be provided by the leader or therapist. Though Adler personally may have believed this as well, most of his group methods were in connection with his community child guidance centers in Vienna, and not in group psychotherapy as such.

The group therapy model that Dreikurs encouraged, where all members of the group are free to say anything they want regarding their own behavior or the behavior of others attending, proved to be the forerunner of the modern group counseling or encounter group movement that literally overwhelmed this country and many other areas of the world a few years ago. Perhaps the supreme irony which emerged from this movement was that most of the encounter groups that were so popular, particularly those conducted by Rogerian and Gestalt schools, though professing to be forums where anyone could express themselves freely, often provided a rather rigid set of rules of behavior and were *less* democratic than the conventional methods of group psychotherapy as practiced by Dreikurs and others who followed him. The essential difference in emphasis by the Gestalt and Rogerian, as opposed to Adler and Dreikurs, is on feelings, not attitude. The discussions must deal with the present and not with the past, and interpretations of motives behind anyone's behavior by any member of the group, including the facilitator, were forbidden. Interestingly enough, in such a process, it was other group members rather than facilitators who punished the offender who violated any of the rules. Research by Yalom [77] and others in the field have indicated that in groups of this nature, the responses to such experiences ranged all the way from wildly enthusiastic to a group of whom at least 10 percent felt that the experience had been damaging or extremely negative to them. Very little followup of the facilitator or therapist was done for those individuals in this 10 percent. Also, as contrasted to the more theraputic model of group psychotherapy, little or no screening was attempted by those who set up such groups to ascertain whether people would likely benefit from the experience.

The more conventional type of group psychotherapy is either carried on in a hospital or clinic setting, or in private psychotherapy practice. Often, the therapist only allows those whom he feels will benefit by the experience to participate in the group sessions. Most of them receive individual therapy as well; and if serious problems develop between the individual and others in the group, the therapist is quick to offer assistance to the individual in private sessions. Screening or followup assistance was not offered in such types of encounter groups.

In relatively unstructured therapy groups, both feelings and attitudes as well as interpretations of an individual's behavior may be presented, either by group members or the leader. For example, in a group that I conducted, one young woman revealed to the group that whenever she was faced with even a minor emotional crisis she would cry. This lack of control, as she expressed it, often caused her great embarrassment, particularly in social situations. When she expressed this to the group, she was relating how she was feeling at the time. However, when efforts were made to ascertain, or at least to have her find out why she would cry rather than react in some other way, the focus became cognitive, or more about finding out the purpose of her behavior. Eventually, the group helped her to realize that crying accomplished two purposes for her. It not only made her feel more helpless, but also obtained sympathy and strokes from others. By developing her thinking through these insights, she was able to reduce the amount of crying except under the most traumatic circumstances, and at the same time, achieve a more positive self-image. Of course, it is obvious that for those individuals who have great difficulty in expressing any kind of feelings, particularly those of anger and fear, either in or outside the group, the encounter group process where feelings are stressed rather than attitudes often could be of great value.

Primarily, this process focuses on the concept that it was not improper to express one's emotions to others, however negative or hostile they may be. However, where the focus was relatively narrow and a need was present, sometimes the facilitator would find it necessary to "rescue" someone from the clutches of the group, when adhering closely to the format could be demanding or intimidating to a person, and now allow a relatively free flow of ideas, whether they be feelings or concepts.

It would seem obvious that both approaches—cognitive group psychotherapy and the encounter group—are helpful to different people in different circumstances. Neither one could be considered useful to everyone, but the differences need to be clarified and understood.

MULTIPLE THERAPY

Though Dreikurs has insisted more than once that his major task was in structuring and redefining Adler's concepts, he developed, or at least recognized early, a number of innovations that at the time were quite daring considering the prevailing psychological climate. Dreikurs's technique of "multiple psychotherapy," as he called it, came about relatively by accident when he found it necessary to train a number of beginning students in therapy at the same time. Because he was such a strong believer in learning by doing, he felt that a much more individualized approach was needed. He and one of his students would first meet a new therapy patient together. After listening to the patient's complaints during the first session, he (or a senior therapist) would meet briefly with the student and discuss what had taken place. The student would then meet the patient on the second session and conduct a diagnostic lifestyle work-up such as described earlier. The student would then make an interpretation of the patient's lifestyle but would not discuss this until the third meeting with the patient. The two therapists would then discuss the patient's problems as revealed by the work-up with, of course, the senior therapist giving his own ideas as to what he observed from the diagnostic work-up. The patient would be asked at appropriate times what he thought of what was being discussed. After a general conclusion had been arrived at by the two therapists, the student would then meet with the patient for subsequent sessions using the agreed-upon format. From time to time, both the patient and the student therapist would meet with the senior therapist to discuss the patient's progress. If it was felt some limitations were needed to be placed on how much of the individual's problems could be revealed to the patient, the two therapists might meet and discuss the work-up before seeing the patient together again. Such a procedure would depend on the severity of the problem, and of course, the extent of training and insights the student had attained at this time.

This was the method by which Dreikurs (in Oregon) introduced me to the art of psychotherapy in 1959. However, I never found out how much help I had provided my patient, a young college undergraduate with whom I met about ten times. After the first multiple session, I at least gained a great deal of insight on how to deal with this young man, as well as with others afterward. One of the values inherent in this method, Dreikurs explained to me, was that the two therapists could very often go much farther in revealing the patient's mistaken perceptions than an individual therapist could in confronting his patient alone. Many variations of this method are possible, but this was the technique Dreikurs utilized in training his students for many years.

PARENT AND TEACHER EDUCATION

Although Dreikurs's initial attempts to apply Adlerian methods directly to the school setting—which were outlined in *Psychology in the Classroom* [30]—were quite successful and amounted to something of a revolution in school practices, unfortunately, even until today, the school climate has been too authoritarian for this revolution to have gained much ground. The violence of the sixties, though commencing primarily in the colleges, infiltrated down into the public schools as well and served mostly to frighten school administrators into trying to maintain even more authoritarian postures than before. This has lasted even into the 1990s, inadequate as it is. At the same time, when Dreikursian principles have been used, they have been found to be highly effective, particularly at the elementary school level, and among ghetto inhabitants. This is described in more detail in the book *Logical Consequences: A New Approach to Discipline* [33].

The Need for Recognition

In his lectures and seminars, Dreikurs was fond of saying that *all* misbehavior results from the need for recognition. I first questioned this as being too all-inclusive, but found that by defining misbehavior as an act the child indulges in repeatedly, even though he knows he is not supposed to do it because it is forbidden by rules set by adult authority, whether justified or not, his major goal nearly always does become a bid to gain recognition from an adult in question and often from others in the classroom as well. More often than not, the results of this kind of behavior often reinforces the child's own impression that he does not get sufficient recognition through positive means and therefore must indulge in misbehavior to get any form of attention—which to him is better than the ultimate penalty of rejection.

The Four Mistaken Goals of Child Behavior

These are (1) attention-getting, (2) power, (3) revenge, and (4) assumed disability. Dreikurs originally called these the four goals of childhood behavior. It is my opinion that this is not entirely definitive because some actions cannot be defined as misbehavior, such as being cooperative solely for the purpose of gaining attention. I also feel there was a fifth goal, that of cooperation or social interest, which might be labeled as a "hoped for" goal. Though Dreikurs never formally admitted that my idea was better, he did not insist that it be removed from our book. The chart on the opposite page was originally designed by Nancy Pearcy of the Corvallis, Oregon, schools in 1968. It describes in relatively simple terms the attitudes and behavior of both the child and the parent in such an encounter, as well as some ways of improving or correcting the situation. By substituting the teacher or any other adult who is dealing with the child, the chart can also be effectively utilized in dealing with cases of classroom misbehavior as well as home misbehavior. In analyzing such a conflict, a very useful method of understanding the goal behind a child's behavior is to review the situation that has occurred by answering the following four questions:

1. How did the child behave? (Or, what did he do?)
2. What did you try to do to correct the behavior?
3. What happened?
4. What was your feeling about the behavior and what was your response as a result of it?

Most interesting, as revealed by the chart, *how the adult feels* at the moment the child indulges in the behavior (a discovery which Dreikurs himself made at the time he was developing this concept) is nearly always a quite accurate indication of which goal the child is attempting to reach. There is also another relatively simple aid in determining whether the goal is attention-getting or power. If the child's goal is attention-getting, and the adult orders him to stop his behavior, if he obeys and waits until the adult parent or teacher has turned his attention elsewhere before repeating the behavior, the goal is usually attention-getting. If the child persists in his misbehavior in defiance of the adult's demand, the goal is obviously power. A very important understanding for the adult to realize in these situations is that in most misbehavior, the basic purpose behind the child's behavior is to involve the adult in some way. The outcome is less important than the process. In a power struggle, for example, most young children are aware they cannot win in the end or gain their way in a particular situation. But merely forcing the adult to try and stop them, in effect, is making the adult do what the child wants. In this way, when children become adolescents, "winning out," even if only temporarily is also much desired. Essentially, most children will settle for the secondary goal of adult involvement because it still represents a measure of control, or in the case of revenge, getting even. Of course, it also gives the child some of the recognition he seeks.

Although each goal is specific to the behavior, the counselor or teacher should also look for a pattern of often repeated behaviors to understand the child's general attitude at the moment. The possibilities are summarized in Table 12.1.

THE MORE SERIOUS GOALS

Though most of the misbehaviors that teachers must deal with—except in inner-city ghettos—have as their goal attention-getting or power, the goal of revenge is

Table 12.1
The Child's Mistaken Goals

Goal of misbehavior	What the child is saying	How parent feels	Child's reaction to reprimand	Corrective measures
Attention-getting	I only count when I am being noticed or served.	Annoyed. Wants to remind. Delighted with "good" child.	Temporarily stops disturbing action when given attention.	Ignore. Answer or do the unexpected. Give attention at pleasant times. Use logical consequences where possible.
Power	I only count when I am dominating, or when you do what I want you to do.	Provoked. Generally wants power. Challenged. "I'll make him do it. He can't get away with it"	Intensifies action when reprimanded. Child wants to win, to be the boss.	Extricate self. Act, not talk. Be friendly. Establish equality. Redirect child's efforts into constructive channels.
Revenge	I can't be liked. I don't have power, but I'll get even with him.	Hurt, mad. "How could he do this to me?"	Wants to get even. Makes self disliked.	Extricate self. Win child. Maintain order with minimum restraint. Take time and effort to help child.
Inadequacy (assumed disability)	I can't do anything right, so I won't try to do anything at all; I'm no good.	Despair. "I give up."	No reprimand, therefore no reaction. Feels there is no use trying. Passive.	Encouragement. (May take a long time). Have faith in child's ability.

Source: Nancy Pearcy. Developed as basis for understanding goals of child behavior during parent study groups. Corvallis, Ore., 1968.

becoming more prevelant and can probably be considered as the motivation behind most crimes of violence today. The news media is full of examples, which
run the gamut from armed robberies, assaults, drive-by shootings, and gang at-
tacks, to individual rapes and murders. Often the term "senseless" or "mindless"
crimes is utilized to describe, for example, a particular incident when an old, helpless woman is beaten and robbed of her purse containing only a few dollars. Of a
similar nature are the inhumanely sadistic methods which some rapists use on

their victims. However bizarre and cruel these acts may seem to the outside observer, they are *not* senseless or mindless, but *purposive acts of revenge*. Such revenge is nearly always a displacement mechanism where the person who commits a "mindless" murder may be getting even with a society which he believes is against him, or parents he believes have rejected or brutalized him. Each time the rapist or torturer assaults his victims, he may be unconsciously revenging himself on his mother or someone in his early childhood by whom he once felt abused. Very often such individuals *have* been abused physically as well as emotionally, although this makes the crimes no less reprehensible or horrifying. Unfortunately, our means of dealing with such people after they have reached adulthood are still tragically inadequate. It is one reason why Adler and Dreikurs, in their late years, moved more and more in their teachings toward preventative methods that emphasized the aspect of therapy rather than merely trying to deal with such aberrations in adult behavior after they have reached the extremes described previously.

THE TECHNIQUE OF ENCOURAGEMENT

Adler stressed repeatedly in all of his forms of counseling and therapy that an essential feature of the role of all counselors, teachers, and parents was to provide encouragement, or positive support of the person in his attempts to correct mistaken perceptions and to adopt cooperative ways of behavior. However, it was Dreikurs who first used the term encouragement as a specific technique, some of the aspects of which he first described in *The Challenge of Parenthood* [29] in 1958. Though at that time it was not given as a systematized theory, encouragement was described as a technique, and was not recognized as merely a general support of any aspects of a child's positive behavior.

In 1961, I was approached by Dreikurs and asked to collaborate with him on a book about encouragement. At the time, I had been working with encouragement and logical consequences as specific techniques with my students in teacher-training courses at San Fernando Valley State College, and my answer to him was that I did not feel there was enough material or enough need for an entire book on encouragement because I found that once my students had learned the fundamental principles, encouragement was not a difficult technique to use. As might have been expected, this answer did not please him at all, and he went to Don Dinkmeyer, whose book on encouragement appeared in 1996. Later, I approached Dreikurs at the First International Adlerian Convention held in Eugene, Oregon, and suggested that we collaborate on a book to be entitled *Logical Consequences* [33]. In my belief, this concept was much more difficult to understand and to administer than was encouragement. Though he still did not agree with my ideas about encouragement, he was most eager to collaborate on such a book and suggested that I begin work on the preliminary draft immediately. One of the major reasons for our difference of opinion was that he felt when adults believed they were encouraging children, too often they were either praising them or rewarding them—neither of which were conducive toward inducing the desired result. In other words, they did not develop the child's own autonomous desire to cooperate, without receiving extrinsic rewards or without being judged as being good or bad for whatever behavior the child manifested. In my teaching I have found that the best way to explain and utilize encouragement is to clearly differentiate between encouragement and reward—particularly those types of rewards that still are practiced by the behaviorists.

Perhaps the most important differences are that the shift in focus should be away from the behavior itself and the result—which in itself might or may not be accompanied by a reward—to the *process*. When a child is rewarded for a positive act by being given a piece of candy, or, in the classroom a gold star, if he is a normal child and reasonably intelligent, he will quickly deduce the purpose of behavior is to gain the reward. Therefore, if no reward is forthcoming, then there is no need to repeat the behavior. A person who encourages, on the other hand, does not offer a specific reward. He merely points out to the child that what he is doing is valuable and should be given favorable recognition. Such terms as, "I like what you have done," "This is a good job," or "You did this much better than before," are typical statements reflecting encouragement. Essentially the focus is on the task being done, not on judging what the person is or is not. Parents and teachers often fall into a judgmental trap by saying, "You are a good boy for doing this." Though, at the time, the child may feel good as a result of this statement, the next time he tries and fails to repeat the success, he may feel that he is bad, and the results are negative even though his failure may not be his own fault. By pointing out the value in what the child is doing, a rewarding situation for him is still present, and no moral judgment is made. The same principle is true when dealing with a child in a situation of logical consequences versus punishment.

There is also another point which needs to be explained about the encouragement process. Even though the adult may have faith that the child can perform a certain task, the child himself cannot feel encouraged until he has done so. Though the existentialists may quarrel with this concept, it is my belief, as it was that of both Adler and Dreikurs, that mere existence is not encouragement in itself. One has to function and cooperate in order to survive. One cannot really feel encouraged unless he has performed a cooperative act.

LOGICAL CONSEQUENCES

Rather interestingly, the term "natural consequences," first described by Herbert Spencer more than one hundred years ago, and alluded to by Rousseau a century earlier, is a term that has been fairly well known. However, Spencer's concept was described primarily to indicate a situation, such as if a child puts his hand on a hot stove and burns it, the shock of such a consequence is sufficient enough to stimulate the child to refrain from touching the stove again. The same would happen if he ran his head into a table—he would then avoid that object thereafter. One of the important aspects of this particular behavior, which appeared to be operating only in human beings or the highest forms of other animals, is that it was usually only necessary to have the consequence occur once for the child to learn not to repeat the act. The behaviorist notion of "extinction" is apparently bypassed in such instances. Though he did not change the term, Spencer also described what Dreikurs later called a "logical" consequence, or a situation where the adult arranges a result that has the same effect, as a natural consequence. Spencer described in his book on education a very good logical consequence that is even usable today. If a young child leaves his toys lying around the house after he is through playing with them, Mother simply put them in a place where he cannot find them. When the child asks for the toys she tells him they were in the way while she was cleaning and she had to put them away, and that the correct place for toys after he is through with them is in his room. When the toys are later returned to him, he at least knows where they belong, and if they again disappear, the consequence becomes more apparent to him.

The essentials of the concept, as has been elaborated in the book *Logical Consequences: A New Approach to Discipline* [33], is that we all experience consequences throughout our lives. Often those that occur as a result of mistaken adult behaviors can be so severe that they emotionally cripple us for life. During the training period, the child or teacher can impose or arrange a result in a child's behavior that may be annoying and distasteful to the child, but not harmful. Often with young children, the first imposition of the consequence may be all that is necessary. If the child persists in the behavior, then the length of time of the consequence can be extended. If a child is playing with other children in a game and is not playing according to rules, the teacher can, for example, say to a child, "Joe, perhaps you better come sit over on the bench because you apparently cannot play the game without following the rules." However, the teacher does not indicate that the child must sit for a specified period of time, which can be considered arbitrary and might nullify the value of the consequence. A few minutes later the teacher could return to the child, saying, "Well, Joe, are you ready to play the game according to the rules?" If he responds, 'Yes," then he is allowed to return to the game. If he still insists on violating the rules, the teacher say, "Well, it looks like you haven't learned to follow the rules yet, so you will have to go back and sit on the bench again." But, this time, the child is required to sit on the bench longer and after each violation of the rules, the time is extended until the child gets the message that if he indulges in a certain behavior, this will be the result.

The superiority of this method over traditional forms of punishment will become quite obvious to the teacher or parent who first utilizes logical consequences successfully. Punishment has been the traditional method used by authority to correct misbehavior including rulers and dictators in keeping their subjects in line, though the severity of such methods has diminished, at least to some extent, in the democratic countries. As a result, punishment has become less effective.

GROUP MARRIAGE COUNSELING

It was during the First International Adlerian Conference, also held in Eugene, Oregon, in 1963, that Dreikurs conducted one of the first marriage counseling interviews ever done in front of a group, which again was another dramatic pioneering effort in this field. Though I was never able to find out what happened to the fortunes of the couple who had been struggling with a therapist to maintain their marriage for two years, the psychologist with whom they had been working (who himself only knew Dreikurs by reputation prior to this meeting) stated after the session that he had learned more about the couple during the hour that Dreikurs counseled them than he had been able to understand during the previous two years he had worked with them.

One of the reasons why Dreikurs was so successful in Oregon, in addition to the many long hours Ray Lowe had spent in laying the groundwork, was that at that time, Freudianism was not as entrenched in Oregon as it was in many other areas of the country.

THE MOVEMENT GROWS

Other highly talented people who were either from Oregon, or were attracted there through the efforts of Dr. Lowe and Dr. Dreikurs, came to these seminars. Among those were Oscar Christiansen, now retired, who conducted courses leading to doctoral degrees in family therapy and teacher education at the University of Arizona, and Maurice Bullard, former Director of Guidance in Corvallis and the organizer of the Oregon Society of Adlerian Psychology. The late Dr. William Pew, who was formerly a pediatrician in Eugene at the time and was so impressed with Dreikurs's ideas that he quit his practice, went to Chicago and obtained his residency in psychiatry, and then with his wife, Miriam, established a training center in Minnesota. Miriam, herself a dynamic and remarkably gifted person, for many years organized a series of parent study groups that supported the several family centers in existence in Eugene, but later went on to obtain her degree in social work, and now conducts lectures and seminars in family counseling all over the country and abroad. There are many others: Harold Kuzuma, who is Director of Continuing Education for the State of Hawaii; Harold McAgbee, former Assistant Superintendent to the Eugene School District and who now teaches at Bowie State University; John Platt, who first studied with Ray Lowe and Rudolf Dreikurs and obtained his degree at the University of Arizona, and is District Psychologist for the Elk Grove School District near Sacramento, California; and Bernice Grunwald, who pioneered the techniques of class group discussions in Chicago and elsewhere. Of course, there are many others not mentioned. The foundation that was laid in Oregon, which though focused to a considerable extent on working with and through the schools, also provided materials and emphasis for a much greatly expanded development of the community child guidance centers, utilizing the Adlerian model that had been previously used. Though the emphasis on psychotherapy has not been neglected, most of the institutes which have developed and many of those who teach at the colleges throughout the country and abroad, have found more support in the field of education than in psychology.

Unfortunately, my own experiences upon returning to Los Angeles from the first summer with Dreikurs were not overly impressive. I was able to start the first family counseling center in the State of California, along Adlerian–Dreikursian lines, and though Dreikurs visited Los Angeles and conducted seminars there a number of times, the response was by no means as enthusiastic as it had been in Oregon, even though by this time he had become accepted and nationally acclaimed. There are a number of reasons for this—the vastness of the population, the distances between schools or centers of learning, and the unique culture of southern California, which has probably spawned more movements of a scientific, religious, or pseudoscientific nature, as well as even sheer cultism, than anywhere else in the world. My counseling families at Prairie Street School in Northridge did, however, make the six o'clock news. Though the results here cannot be measured in terms of numbers, organizations, or institutions, my own teaching was significantly affected by my relationship with Rudolf Dreikurs. Neither of my other books, nor this one, would have been written without my experiences with him.

THE MOVEMENT HERE AND ABROAD

After Oregon, Dreikurs spent less and less of his time in practice and more time in traveling and lecturing as Adler had done before him. The greatest significance was in Dreikurs's return to Europe and Israel, and his many trips back to Germany, Austria, Greece, England, and parts of the United States and Canada. Though essentially his theme was devoted to the areas of psychotherapy, teacher, and parent education, he did move for a time into the area of industrial relations, where he pioneered a concept which was as foreign to collective bargaining as has ever been attempted. His view was that management and labor should work together cooperatively instead of dealing with each other in the conventional adversarial relationship. He used the same approach in attempting to work with the armed forces in Israel at the request of military leaders. He was also tireless in his attempts to develop what he called a "movement," which he felt was the only way ideas could be disseminated on a large enough basis to be significant. In Israel, as a result of his work in labor relations, Dreikurs did formulate four principles of conflict resolution:

1. mutual respect
2. pinpointing the issue
3. mutual agreement
4. shared responsibility

He taught these principles as part of what he considered to be a new technology in human relations. Though he did not live to see them put into effect on a substantial basis, there have been attempts not only in Israel, but many other places in the world, to implement these principles, not only in management and labor disputes, but also in some dialogues between Israelites and Arabs in the Middle East.

The final issue, one that preoccupied him throughout his life, and which for a time he described as a mutual law of life similar to Adler's law of cooperation, was the law of equality, a law that he first felt was beginning to be understood in the United States. But the trend of individualism—the "Me first" doctrine, which seemed to gain a great measure of ascendency in the 1960s—diminished his optimism, but by no means his zeal, in attempting to translate it into reality. Dreikurs's final book, *Social Equality: The Challenge of Our Time* [27], outlines in clear detail the enormous difficulties which we in the United States—who he described as having the most freedom of anyone in the world—are having in coping with the breakdown in authority among parents, schools, and in the community. Until his untimely death in 1972, he continued to emphasize that the methods existed as Adler before him, and he himself had outlined. It was up to all of us to learn to use them efficiently. In the next chapter we will attempt to deal with some of these ideas, particularly as they are applicable to the political and social problems of our day.

Chapter Thirteen

Can Humanity Survive?

To end a book such as this on a political note may seem strange unless one understands that the fate of the world is not in the hands of psychologists, but politicians. Whether any psychological theory becomes persuasive enough to capture the imagination of thinkers the world over, unfortunately it is not they who have the power to promote it. Perhaps an example of what is most recently being promoted is that much is wrong with education here in the United States, but few realize that the solutions, if there are any, are in the hands of those who run school boards, both local and national, and as well the legislators and administrators who control the purse strings that finance education. It is frightening for sure to realize how much our destinies are in the hands of politicians, but except for in dictatorships, they are the people we have chosen to lead and govern us. In a democracy, at least we have the power to throw them out if we do not like what they do. Great movements such as Christianity and Communism, for example, have come from small beginnings, so we may have more to say about what happens than we often admit.

The question posed by this chapter heading has grown visibly in importance as we approach the twenty-first century. The collapse of Communism in Russia has left the world in a state of serious chaos. There are, of course, clear-cut distinctions between democracy and totalitarianism. However, the distinctions between capitalism and socialism—which are the two major economic theories, though theoretically just as diametrically opposed—have become increasingly blurred.

Rudolf Dreikurs once observed that the last 150 years commenced the second great social revolution in human history. In his view, the first began when men and women came out of their caves and formed tribes, then communities, and language was born. This second revolution is, as he stated, the result of technology. Possibly a great deal of the wars today may have resulted from our inability to keep our social developments abreast of our machines.

Along with this has come another development, coping with what has not been easy—freedom, particularly in the United States. There is more freedom here than at any time in our history. Unfortunately, teaching the responsibility that goes along with this has been the greatest failure of our society, both at home and in the schools.

However, I find the underlying problem is more economic than social. The disparity of wealth between the rich and poor is growing here in America as well as in many other developed countries. As the number of poor grow and the middle class diminishes, the anger and frustration have mounted among the less privileged class. This anger has resulted in what can be expected in a free society—more violence between people and more crime in the streets. Added to this is the impossibility of preventing anyone outside of power from attaining a gun—the scenario is not reassuring. The result of this has been legislation for stricter criminal penalties. More persons face the death penalty. Does anyone seriously believe that these are the viable solutions to this problem?

Many well-meaning, but misguided leaders of other cultures view what is happening here as just an aberration particular to our violent nature. But their time will come, and they are already facing some of the problems attributed to growing crime rates that have become endemic here. In some ways, though, we are still inching forward in our understanding of social relations and particularly about what our politicians are doing. One example, Newt Gingrich's "Contract with America" in 1995, is probably as good as any. If passed, those new extreme laws would have gutted our air and water pollution protection, destroyed most federal controls on business, and eliminated welfare benefits to the poor, in the name of "reform." Only the last of these measures passed, and the president signed the so-called "welfare reform" bill reluctantly, simply because in an election year he had to say that he supported such reforms. Some of its provisions and services are seriously chipped away, leaving food stamp distribution in the hands of the states, most of which find ways to cut the benefits, requiring that welfare recipients are arbitrarily cut off if they do not find work in two years—but no real effort has been made to find jobs for these people.

Still, we have free and relatively uncorrupted elections, devoid of the violence that occurs in many of the underdeveloped countries. But the collapse of Communism in Russia has left a void. It is no longer us against them, no longer capitalism against Communism. It is a world struggling to find some semblance of economic security to balance the dramatic increases in the progress of democracy.

Nowhere in the world today can we point to a country and say that their economic and political systems are such that they can be considered a model for all of us to follow. Even Western Europe, which has managed to survive capitalism with a heavy dose of socialistic pills, is suffering—though it must be said that the disparity between rich and poor is smaller in some countries such as Scandinavia and probably Switzerland than anywhere else.

Let us get back to the psychological roots of the problem. Earlier, I talked about three great visionaries who offered answers to our human dilemma: Christ, Marx, and Adler. All three correctly saw in their own ways how the desire for power over others was the ultimate evil and needed to be eliminated. Christ proposed it be done through faith, Marx through imposition of a socialist state, and Adler through self-examination, acceptance of responsibility, and relearning from one's own mistakes.

To date, unfortunately their diagnosis of the human condition appears to have been valid, but their solutions have not worked. Why? In the case of Christ, not enough people are willing to listen and change themselves to solve the world's ills. In the case of Marx, putting that much power in the hands of a few eventually leads to abuses that are more pervasive than the problems sought to eliminate. And yet Marx was even more prophetic than we first thought. If we substitute the word technology for capitalism, his ideals truly mirror the dismal state the world is in today. As long as technology is left in the hands of those who are free to use it only for profit, the world's ills may never be solved.

There are innumerable examples of what technology can do and has done. I can say I would probably not be alive today if not for the miracle of modern medicine, but I can afford it because I have medical insurance.

What few people appear to see in today's world is that the response to technology still only reserved for the few who can afford it, is more crime, more domestic violence, more political and social upheavals, and more so-called "brush fire wars." At least the form of violence has, so far, kept us from a major disaster. However, the missiles are still sitting silently in their silos, while the pace of dismantling them is agonizingly slow.

There are, of course, other movements forward. Not long ago, South Africa ended apartheid—an event no one would have thought possible, even a few years ago, without civil war. We are working toward economic trade agreements which *may* make things easier for more people. Democracy has come to Russia, but how long it will last is anybody's guess.

Along with all this massive progress, we are plundering the world's resources at a staggering rate. Ten to twenty years from now most of the fish not artificially propagated will probably have vanished from the streams, lakes, and oceans. At the same time, most of the rain forests will have been chopped down, global warming is likely to permanently alter the world's climate, and our very existence as human beings may be in great danger.

Perhaps there is consolation in all this. If humanity perishes, the insects will probably take over, particularly the ants, who seem to manage their colonies much more effectively, simply by instinct, than we do.

There are, of course, Huxley's and Orwell's dark solutions to the problem. Is what the world needs a benevolent dictator who will knock our heads together and force us to make changes in order to provide for the poor, and still save our environment in the process? Can we take the risk of setting up such a dictator in advance, when no one can safely predict *before* he assumes power, what he will do after? In this regard, *Brave New World* and *1984* are probably right—finding such a god in the person of one fallible human being is probably impossible. So we muddle along, and where all will end is anybody's guess.

Adler has a viable answer. Having spent nearly fifty years promoting his ideas, I know I influenced a few who benefited from them. Yet, I could never reach even a small fraction of the others. Perhaps this book will help if enough people are persuaded to read it.

One of my friends asked me a very profound question not long ago. "Do you think our knowledge will grow to the extent that we can possibly predict the behavior of a potential criminal when he is still a child?" My answer was no, although some scientists claim to have discovered a gene that causes violent criminality in people. Adler, I think, correctly saw the basis for all human behavior in the fundamental striving for goals, but also realized and stated that nearly all solutions are the result of choices or responses to environmental pressure by individuals. Human beings have such an enormous range of choices that predicting what any one person will *specifically* do, even a year or a few years from now, is virtually impossible. We can see goals and trends and predict great troubles for those with difficulties in their relationships with others, but again, basic change is an iffy matter.

If we can enlist the help of teachers, these changes can do their own miracles with young children if they are reached early enough, so there is always hope. But even in the democracies, particularly here in the United States, most teachers are hemmed in by restrictive and often conflicting political issues foisted upon them by reactionary local school boards and administrators. Even if they had viable solutions to some of these central problems, they might not have the freedom to educate the children. A few—a very select few—have done this in spite of all the hardships and at least have given us a blueprint for the future.

To conclude, all I can say is that the knowledge about how to teach people to replace the drive for power with a desire for love and cooperation has been shown to us by Alfred Adler. Possibly, if mankind becomes sufficiently desperate in the next century, the message will be heard by enough people who will demand that the politicians and dictators make the changes that are needed. The door is still open—for how long no one can really say.

So, it is a race against time—not the time we have invented, but the duration of centuries as Lydia Sicher has called it. Of course, Earth will continue to spin on its axis and wobble uncertainly around the sun for eons to come. But whether it will still be blue, green, and golden as we see it now from space, or a barren deserted wasteland such as that of Mars or Venus, may still be in *our* hands to decide. But not for long. Every day our choices become fewer; the lens aperture narrows even smaller. If we educate our children, it may not yet be too late. If we leave it to our grandchildren and beyond, the lens may be closed forever, and Earth may ultimately become another of the millions of lifeless rocks drifting silently through space, the victim of our experiment with brightened hopes, but which man's greed and lust for power has destroyed.

Epilogue

Among those who contributed greatly to our understanding of Adler, I must again pay tribute to the Ansbachers, whose books have literally become the Bible for those trying to learn more about Adler's ideas. But scholars as they are, the Ansbachers appear to have the same consummate need as most other scholars do. They must examine every statement, every nuance, sometimes every syllable of a particular construct to make sure they have analyzed it completely. Often when one tries to follow this too carefully, one can get lost in the trees.

Though I think the Ansbachers thoroughly understood the scope of Adler's thoughts, they seemed to be more concerned with the psychological details of what he presented, than with the social implications of his system. On the other hand, among a very few, Dreikurs saw the broader meanings behind Adler's views, not only for psychology but for mankind as well, and spent his last years trying desperately to reach as many as he could to disseminate this knowledge.

I hope this book has helped to move this knowledge along. If in this field of psychology, this was the century for Freud, perhaps the twenty-first century will belong to Adler. At least many of his ideas have already been borrowed or stolen by many other disciplines, as I have mentioned. Perhaps now they will come home again, where they belong, so that the full impact and yet unfathomed subtleties of his system will eventually find the acceptance they deserve.

Selected Bibliography

BOOKS BY ALFRED ADLER

1. *A Study of Organ Inferiority and Its Psychological Compensation: A Contribution to Clinical Medicine* (original German, 1907). Trans. S. E. Jellife. New York: Nervous Mental Diseases Publishing Company, 1917.
2. *The Neurotic Constitution: Outline of a Comparative Individualist Psychology and Psychotherapy* (original German, 1912). Trans. B. Glueck and J. E. Lind. New York: Moffat, Yard, 1917.
3. (With Carl Furtmuller.) *Heilen und Bilden: Ärzlich–Pädagogische Arbeiten des Vereins für Individualpsychologie* (Healing and Education: Medical–Educational Papers of the Society for Individual Psychology). Munich: Reinhardt, 1914.
4. *The Practice and Theory of Individual Psychology* (original German, 1922). Trans. P. Radin. London: Routledge and Kegan Paul, 1925.
5. *Understanding Human Nature* (original German, 1927). Trans. Walter B. Wolfe. New York: Greenberg, 1927.
6. *The Case of Miss R: The Interpretation of a Life Story* (original German, 1928). New York: Greenberg, 1929.
7. *Individualpsychologie in der Schule: Vorlesgun für Lehrer und Erziher* (Individual Psychology in the School: Lectures for Teachers and Educators). Leipzig: Hirzel, 1929.
8. *Guiding the Child: On the Principles of Individual Psychology* (original German, 1929). Ed. Alfred Adler, trans. Benjamin Ginzburg. New York: Greenberg, 1930.
9. *Problems of Neurosis: A Book of Case Histories*. Ed. Philip Mairet. London: Routledge and Kegan Paul, 1929.
10. *The Science of Living*. Ed. Benjamin Ginzburg. New York: Greenberg, 1929.
11. *The Education of Children*. Trans. Eleanor and Friedrich Jensen. New York: Greenberg, 1930.
12. *The Pattern of Life*. Ed. Walter B. Wolfe. New York: Greenberg, 1929.

13. *The Problem Child: The Life Style of the Difficult Child as Analyzed in Specific Cases* (original German, 1930). Trans. G. Daniels. New York: Capricorn Books, 1963.
14. *What Life Should Mean to You.* Ed. Alan Porter. Boston: Little, Brown, 1931.
15. (With Ernst Jahn.) *Religion und Individualpsychologie* (Religion and Individual Psychology). Vienna, Leipzig: Passer, 1933. (For partial English translation, see: *Superiority and Social Interest*, 1964.)
16. *Social Interest: A Challenge to Mankind* (original German, 1933). Trans. J. Linton and R. Vaughan. London: Faber & Faber, 1938.

SUPPLEMENTAL REFERENCES

17. Ansbacher, Heinz L., ed. "Alfred Adler: A Preface to the Diary of Vaslav Nijinsky." *The Journal of Individual Psychology* 37 (1981): 131–135.
18. ———, and R. Rowena, eds. *The Individual Psychology of Alfred Adler: A Systematic Presentation in Selections from His Writings.* New York: Basic Books, 1956.
19. ———. *Superiority and Social Interest: A Collection of Later Writings.* Evanston, Ill.: Northwestern University Press, 1964.
20. ———. *Cooperation between the Sexes.* Garden City, N.Y.: Doubleday, 1978.
21. Aserinsky, E., and N. Kleitman. "Regularly Occurring Periods of Eye Motility and Concomitant Phenomena during Sleep." *Science* 118 (1953): 273–274.
22. Brachfeld, Oliver. *Inferiority Feelings in the Individual and the Group.* New York: Grume & Stratten, 1951.
23. Cannon, Walter B. *The Wisdom of the Body.* New York: W. W. Norton, 1932.
24. Cartwright, Rosalind A. Article 3 in *The Meaning of Dreams: Recent Thoughts from the Laboratory.* State of California, Department of Mental Hygiene Symposium, 1969.
25. Christiansen, Oscar C. *Adlerian Family Counseling.* Minneapolis: Educational Media, 1993.
26. Cassidy, David. *The Life and Science of Werner Heisenberg.* New York: W. H. Freeman, 1992.
27. Dreikurs, Rudolf. *Social Equality: The Challenge of Our Time.* Chicago: Adler School of Professional Psychology, 1972.
28. ———. *The Challenge of Marriage.* New York: Penguin Books, 1965.
29. ———. *The Challenge of Parenthood.* New York: Penguin Books, 1958.
30. ———. *Psychology in the Classroom.* New York: Harper & Row, 1957.
31. ———, Ray Lowe, and Bina Rosenberg. *Manual of Adlerian Family Counseling.* Eugene, Ore.: University of Oregon Press, 1959.
32. ———, and Vicki Stoltz. *Children the Challenge.* New York: Duell, Sloane & Pierce, 1964.
33. ———, and Loren Grey. *Logical Consequences: A New Approach to Discipline.* New York: Meredith Press, 1968.
34. ———. *Discipline Without Tears.* New York: Hawthorne Books, 1973.
35. ———, and Loren Grey. *A Parents' Guide to Child Discipline.* New York: Hawthorne Books, 1970.
36. ———, Ray Corsini, Floy Pepper, and Bernice Grunwald. *Maintaining Sanity in the Classroom.* New York: Harper & Row, 1971.
37. Ellis, Albert. *Inside Rational–Emotive Therapy.* San Diego: Advance Press, 1985.
38. Foulkes, David, and E. Fromm. *The Psychology of Dreams.* New York: Charles Scribner's Sons, 1966.

39. French, Thomas S., and E. Fromm. *Dream Interpretation.* New York: Basic Books, 1969.
40. Glasser, William. *Reality Therapy.* New York: Harper & Row, 1965.
41. Greenberg, R. *Dream Deprivation Study.* A report to the Association for the Psychological and Physiological Study of Sleep. Gainsville, Fla.: 1966.
42. Guiley, Rosemary Ellen. *The Encyclopedia of Dreams.* New York: Berkeley Books, 1993.
43. Haley, Jay. *Techniques of Family Therapy.* New York: Harcourt Brace, 1956.
44. Harlow, Harry. "The Nature of Love." *The American Psychologist* 3 (1958): 173–185.
45. Heisenberg, Werner. *On Modern Physics.* Ed. David Bohm. New York: Clarkson Potter, 1961.
46. Hoffman, Edward. *The Drive for Self: Alfred Adler and the Fundamentals of Individual Psychology.* Reading, Mass.: Addison-Wesley, 1994.
47. Kohler, Wolfgang. *The Place of Value in a World of Facts.* New York: Liverwright, 1938.
48. Krech, David, and R. S. Crutchfield. *Theory and Problems in Social Psychology.* New York: McGraw Hill, 1948.
49. James, William. *Pragmatism: A New Name for Some Old Ways of Thinking.* New York: Longmans Green, 1907.
50. Jensen, Arthur H. *Bias in Mental Testing.* New York: Free Press, 1980.
51. Jones, Richard M.. *The New Psychology of Dreaming.* New York: Grune & Stratten, 1970.
52. Lowy, Samuel. *Psychological and Biological Foundation of Dream Interpretation.* London: Routledge and Kegan-Paul, 1942.
53. Maslow, A. H. *Motivation and Personality.* New York: Harper & Row, 1959.
54. ———. "Self-Actualization: A Study of Pyschological Health." Personality Symposiums, vol 1. New York: 1958.
55. Masters, William H., and Virginia Johnson. *Human Sexual Responses.* Toronto: Bantam Books, 1980.
56. McCarley, Robert. "Dream Study." *American Journal of Psychiatry* 14 (1977).
57. Peat, F. David. *Infinite Potential: The Life and Times of David Bohm.* Reading, Mass.: Addison-Wesley, 1997.
58. Perls, Fritz. *Gestalt Therapy. Verbatim.* Salt Lake City: Real People Press, 1969.
59. Piaget, Jean. *Equibrilation of Cognitive Structures: The Central Problem of Intellectual Development.* Chicago: University of Chicago Press, 1985.
60. Rogers, Carl. *Client-Centered Therapy: Its Current Practice, Implications and Theory.* Boston: Houghton Mifflin, 1951.
61. Satir, Virginia. *Conjoint Family Therapy.* New York: Science & Behavior, 1967.
62. Selye, Hans. *The Stress of Life.* New York: McGraw Hill, 1976.
63. Sheldon, G. M. *Varieties of Temperament.* New York: Harper & Row, 1942.
64. Shockley, William B. *The Eugenics of Race.* Washington, D.C.: Scott Townsend, 1992.
65. Sicher, Lydia. *Collected Works.* Ed. Adele Davidson. Fort Bragg, Calif.: Q.E.D. Press (1920), 1991.
66. Smuts, J. C. *Holism and Evolution* (1920). New York: Viking Press, 1961.
67. Snyder, Frederick. "Progress in the New Biology of Dreaming." *American Journal of Psychiatry* 122 (1965): 377–391.
68. Snygg, D., and A. W. Combs. *Individual Behavior: A New Frame of Reference.* New York: Harper & Row, 1949.

69. Spiel, Oscar, and Ferdinand Biernbaum. *Disciplining Without Punishment: Account of a School in Action.* London: Faber & Faber, 1962.
70. Stewart, Kilton. "Dream Theory in Malaysia," in *Altered States of Consciousness.* Key West, Fla., 1969.
71. Sulloway, Frank. *Born to Rebel.* New York: Pantheon Books, 1996.
72. Turner, Janet, and William Pew. *The Courage to Be Imperfect: The Life and Work of Rudolf Dreikurs.* New York: Hawthorne Books, 1970.
73. Ullman, Montague. "Dreaming, Lifestyle & Psychology: A Comment on Adler's View of the Dream." *The Journal of Individual Psychology* 18 (1962): 18–25.
74. Vaihinger, Hans. *The Philosophy of "As If": A System of the Theoretical, Practical, and Religious Fictions of Mankind.* New York: Harcourt Brace, 1925.
75. Wertheimer, Max. *Productive Thinking.* New York: Harper & Row, 1945.
76. Wexberg, Erwin. *Individual Psychology.* New York: Greenberg, 1923.
77. Yalom, A. *The Theory and Practice of Group Psychotherapy.* New York: Basic Books, 1995.

SUPPLEMENTAL BOOKS BY LOREN GREY

78. *Discipline Without Tyranny: Child Training in the First Five Years.* New York: Hawthorne Books, 1972.
79. *Discipline Without Fear: Child Training During the Early School Years.* New York: Hawthorne Books, 1974.

Index

ABOUT THE AUTHOR

LOREN GREY is Professor Emeritus of Educational Psychology at California State University, Northridge. A past Associate Editor of the *Journal of Individual Psychology* and a former director of the San Fernando Valley Educational Center, Grey has published widely, including, with Dr. Rudolf Dreikurs, *Logical Consequences: A New Approach to Discipline* (1968) and *A Parent's Guide to Child Discipline* (1970) and, on his own, *Discipline Without Tyranny: Child Training in the First Five Years* (1972) and *Discipline Without Fear: Child Training During the Early School Years* (1974).